The Royal Yacht
Britannia

Third Edition

H.M.Y. BRITANNIA

THE ROYAL YACHT BRITANNIA

INSIDE THE QUEEN'S FLOATING PALACE

THIRD EDITION

BY

BRIAN HOEY

Patrick Stephens Limited

AN IMPRINT OF HAYNES PUBLISHING

First published in 1995
Second edition 1998
Third edition 1999

A catalogue record for this book is
available from the British Library

ISBN 1 85260 601 0

Library of Congress catalog
card no. 99-71544

Haynes North America Inc.,
861 Lawrence Drive, Newbury Park,
California 91320, USA

Patrick Stephens Limited is an imprint
of Haynes Publishing, Sparkford,
Nr Yeovil, Somerset BA22 7JJ, UK

Tel: 01963 440635 Fax: 01963 440001
Int.tel: +44 1963 440635
Int.fax: +44 1963 440001

E-mail: sales@haynes-manuals.co.uk
Web site: http://www.haynes.com

Designed and typeset by
G&M, Raunds, Northamptonshire
Printed and bound in England by
J. H. Haynes & Co. Ltd

CONTENTS

A blizzard-bound Royal Yacht waits for her orders to proceed to warmer climes.

Author's Note

H.M.Y. BRITANNIA

ON 11 DECEMBER 1997 Her Majesty's Yacht *Britannia* decommissioned in Portsmouth in the presence of The Queen, Prince Philip, and other members of the Royal Family. The decision to end the 43-year life of *Britannia* was announced in Parliament on 23 June 1994 by the then Secretary of State for Defence, Mr Malcolm Rifkind when he said:

HM Royal Yacht was launched in 1953 and commissioned for service in January 1954 . . . Since then she has travelled over one million miles and has served as a Royal residence and a setting for official entertainment by The Queen and members of the Royal Family during State and other visits overseas and in home waters, and has also been used for the promotion of British commercial interests overseas.

She was originally designed to have the additional function of serving as a hospital ship in time of war, but has never served in this capacity and it is no longer practicable for her to do so. Her outstanding contribution over the years reflects the great care and professionalism which the Royal Navy, and in particular her successive ship's companies, have devoted to her.

The Yacht last underwent a major refit in 1987. A further refit at an estimated cost of some £17 million would be necessary in 1996–97 but would only prolong her life for a further five years . . . It has therefore been decided to decommission *Britannia* in 1997 . . . The Queen has made it known that in the light of changes in the pattern of Royal visits since the Yacht was built, she does not consider a Royal Yacht to be necessary in future solely for the purposes of Royal travel.

With these words the Government announced the ending of a British maritime tradition that began in the 17th century when Charles II ordered his first Royal Yacht, and continued with every succeeding Monarch since then.

In this second edition I have brought right up to date the story of *Britannia* which was started while she was a seagoing Royal Yacht. Until the final moment of decommission this is told in the present tense, which is how the Yacht's many thousands of admirers worldwide would like to remember *Britannia* – in their hearts still alive, lovingly maintained, and playing her role as the most romantic and glamorous of all Royal residences.

ACKNOWLEDGEMENTS

MY FIRST EXPRESSION of appreciation must go to Her Majesty The Queen who gave me permission to go on board her Royal Yacht and view the State Apartments.

When the idea of this book was being discussed I was encouraged by Charles Anson, then Press Secretary to The Queen, and John Haslam, at that time, Deputy Press Secretary. Since then Geoffrey Crawford, the present Press Secretary, has been of great help, and others in the Buckingham Palace Press Office, Felicity Murdo-Smith, and Penny Russell-Smith, were equally generous with their time and expertise. My thanks also to Lady Sheila de Bellaigue and Gwyneth Campling at Windsor Castle.

I am glad to be able to record my thanks to Captain Peter Voute RN (Retd) and Captain Christopher Esplin-Jones RN, former Director of Public Relations, Royal Navy, Ministry of Defence. Rear-Admiral Sir Robert Woodard, former Flag Officer Royal Yachts, provided me with hospitality on board *Britannia* and also contributed greatly to the text through personal interviews.

Commander Paul Jackson was the conduit through which I was able to visit the Yacht and talk to members of the crew. I am grateful for his patience and good humour. Similarly, Commander 'Rick' Cosby opened many doors on board and gave me first-hand accounts of life as an officer serving on *Britannia*. Lieutenant Commander Bob Henry, as Keeper and Steward of the Royal Apartments, spent many hours briefing me on his role and proved to be an excellent tour guide through the Royal Apartments, while David 'Snaps' Hunt, the Yacht's photographer, went to endless trouble to make sure I had the pictures I needed. I would also like to express my thanks to Commander Rupert Head. Many thanks to them and to the other members of the Yacht's complement without whose co-operation this book would not have been possible. All pictures credited HM Yacht are © Crown Copyright/MOD. Reproduced with the permission of the Controller of HMSO.

Rear-Admiral Sir John Garnier, KCVO, CBE, provided all the information about the evacuation from Aden, while Rear-Admiral Sir Paul Greening, GCVO, Major General Sir Simon Cooper, KCVO, Michael Jephson, MVO, and Michael Parker, MVO, arranged for me to be present at a Sea Day and explained to me their various roles.

I would also like to thank Flora Myer, who 'drove' the project through to its conclusion.

PROLOGUE

*B*RITANNIA WAS THE last ship in the Royal Navy in which the sailors slept in hammocks; she is the only ship in the world whose Captain, by tradition, was always an Admiral. This was the case from her commissioning in 1954 through until April 1995, when for the first time a Commodore was appointed as Commander.

Nowhere on her hull will you find her name and yet she is the most easily recognised craft afloat. Her decks are made of teak from the forests of Burma, she has criss-crossed the earth seven times, and even though she is now more than 40 years old she is still running on her original engines.

Britannia is manned for her role by 21 officers and 256 Yachtsmen (called Yotties), plus a small Royal Marine Band of 26 – but no chaplain.

The ship's company wear soft-soled plimsoles at all times and orders are given by hand signal to preserve the tranquillity required in a Royal residence. Shouting is forbidden. She is equipped with the latest satellite communications systems and on the Royal Bridge a special mahogany windbreak has been built to prevent any sea breezes from blowing up the Royal skirts.

Britannia is an independent command in the Royal Navy. This means she does not answer to any of the recognised fleets and is the only ship in which there is no set punishment routine. They do not have 'Defaulters'. If anyone deserves punishment he is immediately banished as being unfit to serve.

She carries her own non-profit making 24-hour laundry, a garage for the Royal Rolls-Royce (last used over 20 years ago) and when she is in port no member of the crew is permitted to go ashore unless he is wearing a tie. Officers wear stiff white collars and formal uniform at all times. The loyal toast is drunk standing up – again the only ship in the Navy in which this tradition is followed.

She has been used for four Royal honeymoons – and all four of the couples have since split up, so her (below decks) nickname of 'the Love Boat' is no longer entirely appropriate. Noel Coward has played the drawing room piano, Sir Hugh Casson designed the interior – and then had to argue for his fee – and some of the furniture on board was designed by Prince Albert back in 1856. The corridor where the senior officers' cabins are located is called the 'Whispering Gallery', while the tiny cubby holes where the junior officers live are known as the 'Ghetto'.

The State Dining Room doubles as a

Britannia lying in front of the Royal Naval College at Dartmouth, where so many of her officers began their careers, including every one of the men who have commanded the Royal Yacht.

church and conference hall, while among the treasures on board are a fragment of a tattered white ensign flown on Scott of the Antarctic's sledge and removed in 1912 when his body was recovered. There is also a gold button from the tunic of Admiral Lord Nelson.

The Queen says that *Britannia* is the one place in the world where she can truly relax and it is, in fact, her Palace afloat. The ship is as much a Royal home as Buckingham Palace, Windsor Castle, Holyrood House, Balmoral or Sandringham.

She is undoubtedly the smartest ship in the world, a picture of perfection, the envy of presidents and potentates and without doubt, the pride of the seven seas.

This is her story.

INTRODUCTION

AT PRECISELY HALF past two in the afternoon of Thursday, 16 April 1953, The Queen stood on a raised platform high above the shipyard of John Brown & Co. Ltd in Glasgow. She was presented with a bouquet of flowers by Miss Robin Bullard, a granddaughter of the Chairman, and Her Majesty, after uttering the obligatory few words about blessing all who sail in her, then pressed a button, which released a metal arm containing a bottle of Empire wine (no champagne, this still being the age of post-war austerity when food, sweets and clothes were rationed in Britain). The wine was duly smashed against the bow of the new Royal Yacht – which she named *Britannia*.

The name of the yacht had been kept a secret for many months. It was chosen personally by Her Majesty from a list containing dozens of suggestions. So secret was the final selection that the invitations to guests attending the launching ceremony omitted the name and merely said:

The invitation to the launch of the as yet un-named yacht.

> *Her Majesty The Queen,*
>
> *having graciously consented to name and launch*
>
> *Her Majesty's Yacht*
>
> *at Clydebank Shipyard*
>
> *on Thursday, Sixteenth April 1953. at 2.15 p.m.*
>
> *The Chairman and Directors of*
>
> *John Brown and Company Limited*
>
> *request the honour of the company of*
>
> *The Rt. Hon. J. P. L. Thomas M.P.*
>
> *to witness the Ceremony*
>
> *R.S.V.P*
> *on the enclosed card*

HER MAJESTY THE QUEEN
having graciously consented to name
and launch
HER MAJESTY'S YACHT
at Clydebank Shipyard
on Thursday Sixteenth April 1953
at 2.15 p.m.

Until the moment of launching, the Royal Yacht was known simply as ship number 691 and, initially contract number CP8/50839/52/V.91. That was the number allocated by the Director of Navy Contracts at the Admiralty when John Brown & Co. Ltd. of Clydebank,

Glasgow, were awarded the contract on 5 February 1952 – the day before King George VI died and his daughter became Queen Elizabeth II.

Britannia was an appropriate choice of name even if it came as a complete surprise to the waiting public and to the Press covering the event. For months bookmakers had been laying odds on what the new Royal Yacht was to be called: *The Elizabeth* was a favourite, while *George & Elizabeth* (in tribute to The Queen's late father), *Elizabeth &* *Philip* and *Elizabeth II* all had their supporters. But The Queen had done her homework and she knew that this was a proud maritime name with a long and distinguished naval pedigree and the final decision was hers and hers alone. *Britannia* was also the name of the most successful of all Royal sailing yachts, being owned in turn by King Edward VII and King George V.

The new *Britannia* was to become the most famous of them all. She would steam more than a million miles in her

She would become the most famous Britannia *of them all, sailing more than one million miles as one of the most majestic symbols of British sovereignty . . .*

lifetime, carrying The Queen and her family on colourful voyages to Africa, the West Indies, Australia and New Zealand. She would cruise up the St. Lawrence Seaway to the Great Lakes of Canada and visit both east and west coasts of the United States. She would carry the flag to the South China Seas, the Adriatic and the Mediterranean.

Presidents and Prime Ministers would dine on board. Kings and Queens would marvel at her sumptuous State Apartments. Privy Councils would be held on board; men would be knighted, and she would prove herself under fire in the Red Sea. Royal honeymoons would be spent in this most romantic of all Royal residences – and The Queen would come to say, 'This is where I can truly relax'.

. . . She would carry the flag to the South China Seas, the Adriatic, and the Mediterranean. (Photographers International)

A Day in the Life Of...

ALTHOUGH THE QUEEN herself claims that *Britannia* is the one place in the world where she can really be at ease, it is never all pleasure for her. Her routine rarely alters, even on board, and she is never far from one of her Private Secretaries, with a mass of paperwork demanding her attention.

At 7.30 every morning she is woken by her personal maid who brings in the early morning tea – a special blend made solely for Her Majesty by

Whenever Her Majesty embarked or disembarked, the Flag Officer Royal Yachts was present in full ceremonial uniform complete with sword and telescope. Admiral Woodard's tropical white denotes the fine weather in the French port of Bordeaux in the summer of 1992. (Courtesy H.M. Yacht)

The Queen has often told friends that Britannia is the only place where she can truly relax. Even at Balmoral and Sandringham it is difficult for her to get away from everyone. Here she is left completely alone when she wants to be, and that is why she loves it so.

Twinings of The Strand in London. The tea is served with milk but no sugar. The maid draws back the curtains on the large porthole windows which are situated higher than normal so that nobody passing on the deck outside is able to see in.

The Queen's bathroom adjoins her bedroom cabin and there is a thermometer there to ensure that the water is exactly the right temperature. Her Majesty makes no secret of the fact that she prefers a bath. Prince Philip nearly always takes a shower.

Meanwhile, Prince Philip, in his bedroom cabin next door, is drinking the first of several cups of coffee he will consume during the next hour or so. He likes it black with no sugar and again it is a special blend made for the Royal Family; by the Savoy Hotel coffee department.

After having breakfast on the Verandah Deck, The Queen returns to her sitting room, never later than 9.15 a.m. to start work on her 'boxes' – the ever present containers from various Government departments which arrive every morning with official documents. These boxes follow her around the world and she works for several hours with her Private Secretary, Sir Robert Fellowes, before breaking for coffee at 11 a.m.

This is when the menus for that evening's dinner are offered for her approval. There is usually a choice of three. Her Majesty will tick which ones she prefers – though occasionally she

Even on holiday The Queen spends several hours every day working on official papers from all over the Commonwealth.
(David Secombe)

will decline all three and make suggestions of her own. At sometime during the morning, the Commander of the Royal Yacht will present his compliments and inform Her Majesty of *Britannia's* present position and the distance she has travelled overnight.

Lunch on board is normally a buffet which is served in the dining room. Other members of the Royal Family will join The Queen from whatever activity they have been doing during the morning. The Duke of Edinburgh also uses the morning period for paperwork, keeping the afternoons for his favourite shipboard hobbies of painting and reading.

After lunch the family disperses again with The Queen using the time for private correspondence. On the Western Isles cruise during the summer she spends several afternoons signing some of the hundreds of Christmas cards she and the Duke send out each year. They do not sign them together; The Queen signs first and they are then passed to His Royal Highness to add his signature. This is something he has to be per-

suaded to do as, like many men, he finds the chore of writing his own name over and over again tedious and boring.

At five o'clock in the afternoon, everything on board the Royal Yacht stops for tea, one of the most immutable of all Royal traditions. At sea or ashore, it is always the same: Wafer-thin cucumber and salmon sandwiches, pastries and gateaux, with the tea served in the finest bone china cups, all bearing the Royal Cypher.

Once tea is finished, Her Majesty retires to her bedroom where she will spend some time with her two dressers – whose cabins are on the same deck – checking her wardrobe, and, if there is to be a formal function, which items from her jewellery collection she intends to wear that evening.

Dinner is the most important meal of the day. The Queen always changes for it even if it is during one of the holiday cruises when only the family is present and dress is fairly casual.

The family gather in the ante-room at 7.30 p.m. for drinks, when they may be joined by the Commander of the Yacht

The Foreign Office and the Department of Trade and Industry are convinced that they are able to attract enormous benefits to British industry. Working on the basis that very few people will turn down an invitation to spend a day on the most famous ship in the world, it gives them a platform on which to build contacts at the highest level.

and perhaps one or two of his officers. During the Western Isles cruise each officer can expect to be invited to dine at least once with The Queen and Prince Philip.

The senior members of the Household, including the Ladies-in-Waiting, who are more like companions than servants, sometimes eat with The Queen. Otherwise they have their own dining room or take some of their meals in the Ward Room at the invitation of the Yacht's officers.

Family dinner is served on green and white Spode china decorated with the Royal Cypher. The Queen sits on the starboard side of the mahogany dining table. She uses a small bell to let the stewards know when a course has to be cleared away and in this way, the staff can leave the Royal Family in complete privacy during the meal.

If any of the younger children in the Royal Family are on board they will eat separately from the adults, but with almost as much preparation and under strict supervision, so that by the time they are ready to join the senior members of the family at meals, they are fully aware of the protocol involved and how to behave properly. Royal training begins at a very early age.

Depending on where *Britannia* is and the weather at the time, Royal meals may sometimes be taken ashore. The Queen enjoys picnics and Prince Philip and the Princess Royal love barbecues, so occasionally *Britannia* will anchor in a secluded spot and after a 'recce' by one of the yacht's officers and The Queen's police officer to find a suitable site, they will all troop ashore. There they are left in comparative peace and quiet – apart from the

Prince Philip and his Uncle Dickie (Earl Mountbatten of Burma) relax just before landing in the Fiji Islands. Lord Mountbatten was a frequent passenger on Britannia – *and he loved every minute of it.* (Courtesy of the Broadlands Archives)

policemen who watch from a discreet distance.

Prince Philip is the most accomplished outdoor cook in the family — though sometimes with surprising results. He once prepared something for The Queen that was not quite right and she spent the remainder of the day in her cabin.

Once dinner is over, The Queen and her family move into the Drawing Room for coffee and her favourite chocolate mints. Then, after the Dining Room has been cleared it is converted into a private cinema and one of the latest Hollywood blockbusters is shown. James Bond movies are very popular and action films are generally preferred to those of a quieter character.

Drinks are served before the film starts. When Lord Mountbatten was alive he would often keep up a running commentary during the film, especially if it was a war story. After the film ends, it's back to the Drawing Room for a nightcap and perhaps a half hour on one of the giant jigsaw puzzles that are nearly always on the go when The Queen is on board.

And as is the custom in every Royal residence, nobody goes to bed until Her Majesty retires for the night. But on the Royal Yacht late nights are usually reserved for when a formal function is being held. Things are normally quiet long before midnight. But it is sometimes possible to see a light in The Queen's cabin as she works late into the night on documents that need urgent attention. Even on board ship, the business of Monarchy never stops.

THE STATE APARTMENTS

BRITANNIA IS A combination of palace, private yacht and country house and is, in fact, two ships in one.

Forward of the funnel, or 'chimney' as the crew call it, is 'HMS Britannia' – the Royal Navy side of the ship where all the operational equipment and the men required to run it are located. Here it looks exactly like any of the 'grey' warships of the fleet – austere, functional and, apart from the Commodore's cabin,

somewhat cramped. In fact, a typical service vessel.

Aft of the 'chimney' is Her Majesty's Yacht Britannia, containing the luxurious living quarters of the Royal Family and the sumptuous State Apartments.

Moving through the solid steel doors that divide the naval end from the yacht end is to enter another world. The bustle of everyday life below decks is replaced by a calm, dignified atmos-

From her external appearance it is difficult to realize that Britannia *is in fact two ships in one – a functional vessel of the Royal Navy and a sumptuous Royal residence.* (Courtesy H.M. Yacht)

The Drawing Room is furnished in typical 'country house' style – chintz covered armchairs and sofas, with a magnificent carpet, one of two given to The Queen by the Gulf States. (Courtesy H.M. Yacht)

phere in which it is not in the least bit difficult to imagine one is in a Royal residence.

At Buckingham Palace, Windsor Castle or Sandringham, you get the impression that whatever happens outside, here life proceeds at an orderly pace, with never a need for speed. The idea of anyone running or shouting would seem unthinkable. Similarly, on board *Britannia*, at least in this aft part, the atmosphere is relaxed, unhurried and peaceful. The furnishings and decor of the Royal apartments convey a feeling of country house comfort rather than formal elegance. And while it is true that they are elegant, there is not the slightest hint of ostentation anywhere in The Queen's apartments. Everything looks as if it has been there for years, which in most cases it has. The royal tradition of never throwing anything away and making use of old and, in

some cases much loved, items, is displayed throughout *Britannia*, with many of the pictures, furniture and even bed-clothes, coming from previous Royal Yachts.

When *Britannia* was being equipped, back in 1953, the sheets and blankets for The Queen's bedroom came from the old *Victoria & Albert*. Some of them were very ancient indeed and a directive from the Admiralty instructed the then Keeper and Steward of the Royal Apartments to sell those that were too far gone to be repaired. Eventually, 24 blankets were sold at five shillings (25p)

The idea of a hospital ship was not just a sop to public opinion but a realistic approach to the problem of combining the needs of the Royal Navy with those of the Royal Family.

each. Had anyone had the foresight to buy the lot and preserve them, they would have proved a good investment as royal souvenirs.

What the designers have tried, and indeed succeeded in doing, is to convey an atmosphere of restrained good taste and at the same time, by combining artifacts from previous royal yachts with items personally chosen by The Queen, make her and her family feel at home, no matter where they may be in the world.

The Queen's Drawing Room is approached via a small but useful ante-room where a bar is set up before lunch and dinner. There Her Majesty and her family gather for drinks before they move into the dining room. The ante-room is divided from the Drawing Room by a full-length mahogany folding door. This is left open more often than not, so that both rooms appear to be one large, single unit.

The ante-room contains a number of items brought from the last Royal Yacht. There is a fine mahogany book case and sideboard which were originally in the King's study on board the *Victoria & Albert* and inside it are a glass salver, a goblet and a number of glasses in Waterford crystal which were presented to The Queen by John Brown and Co., the builders of the yacht, when *Britannia* was launched.

There is a tradition that when Royal Yachts are being built a number of coins, minted in the same year, are placed beneath the masts for good luck. When the *Victoria & Albert* was broken up in 1955, two sovereigns, one half sovereign, three five shilling pieces, one half crown and two pennies, dated 1899, were recovered and these now rest in the bookcase. Queen Victoria had placed one sovereign, one five shilling

The combined suite of ante-room and Drawing Room where the floor to ceiling doors are usually left open to create one large single unit. (Courtesy H.M. Yacht)

The view from the ante-room in the old days, showing the dividing doors half closed. This is where the Royal Family likes to play cards or complete a jigsaw puzzle. (Courtesy of the late Sir Hugh Janion)

The ante-room contains a fine mahogany bookcase which was originally in the King's study on board the old Victoria & Albert. *Inside are crystal goblets presented to The Queen by the builders of* Britannia. *(Courtesy H.M. Yacht)*

piece and one penny, while King Edward VII (then Prince of Wales) placed the same amount, and King George V (then Duke of York) placed one half sovereign, one five shilling piece and a half crown. At *Britannia's* launching in 1953, coins were placed under the heel of each of her masts, and these will remain there until she too is disposed of.

An attractive model of a former Royal Yacht in a glass case is also dated 1899. The solid silver model of *Britannia* was a present to Her Majesty from the Chairman of Lloyds Register of Shipping in June 1972.

Pride of place on one wall is given to a small, tattered piece of silk in a picture frame. It is part of the white ensign flown on Captain Scott's sledge during his ill-fated Polar expedition and was removed in 1912 when his body was found. The ensign was given to King George V by Commander Evans (Evans of the 'Broke and a member of Scott's team) in 1913.

The miniature White Ensign that was flown on Captain Scott's sledge during his Polar expedition. It was recovered, along with his body, in 1912, and offered to King George V the following year. (Courtesy H.M. Yacht)

The ante-room contains a mixture of fairly old and comparatively modern furniture. The older items came from the *Victoria & Albert*, while most of the newer furniture is Swedish and was a gift to The Queen from the Swedish Royal Family in 1956.

In the left-hand corner of the Drawing Room as you enter is a Walmar baby grand piano. This is fastened to the

This satinwood desk was used frequently by Queen Victoria on her Royal Yacht the Victoria & Albert. *The clock is of more recent vintage and was a present to The Queen in 1991. (Courtesy H.M. Yacht)*

floor by bolts, in case it might take off in bad weather. When The Queen decided she wanted a piano in her Drawing Room the original estimates for furnishing the yacht were amended to include the cost of a grand piano at £350. It was a very reasonable price even in those days but the suppliers were happy to provide the instrument for this sum even though it meant they would not be making a penny profit out of the transaction.

The same thing happened with the radiogram. That cost £170, an enormous amount in 1952, when a family saloon car could be bought for less than £500. The radiogram obviously outlived its usefulness many years ago and was removed. For some years the piano stood on the opposite side, until the Duke of Edinburgh, with his ever practical eye, realised that the way it was positioned meant that the straight edge of the instrument cut off a significant area of the room, thereby reducing the amount of space, so he had it moved.

NO SUCH THING AS A FREE MEAL

Princess Alexandra, the Princess of Wales and Princess Margaret are the most accomplished pianists in the Royal Family and they occasionally like to play when they are on board. If The Queen is giving a reception she will sometimes order the resident pianist with the Royal Marines Band to tinkle away discreetly. The repertoire is strictly 'middle of the road' – Cole Porter, Gershwin, the occasional Andrew Lloyd Webber, but nothing classical and never Rock 'n' Roll. Perhaps the most celebrated performer on this piano was Sir Noel Coward who was invited to dinner on board by Princess Margaret during a Caribbean cruise. He literally 'sang for

The Princess of Wales chose all their meals in consultation with the Royal chef, and as they were sailing in temperatures of around 90 degrees Fahrenheit, most of it was cold food, with ice cream served as dessert after nearly every meal.

his supper', playing many of his own compositions into the wee small hours. Even on the Royal Yacht there is no such thing as 'a free meal'.

The Drawing Room is furnished with comfortable chintz-covered sofas and deep armchairs. The silver grey carpet which runs through the entire length of the Royal deck is partly covered by two magnificent Persian rugs, gifts from two of the Gulf States visited by The Queen in 1979. The one you step on as you enter the room came from Bahrain and the other, nearest the fireplace, from Dubai. A third Persian rug covers the floor of the ante-room.

The fireplace itself is worthy of mention. When *Britannia* was being designed it was originally intended that there would be a working open fireplace in the Drawing Room to make The Queen feel at home. There was nothing in maritime regulations to prevent this. In fact, both Queen Victoria and King Edward VII insisted on coal fires in their yachts. However, it was discovered that there was, and still is, a Royal Navy rule which states that any ship in which an open fire is kept must also have a sailor, complete with fire bucket, standing by the fireplace at all times. As this would have rather defeated the object, the idea of a log or coal fire was quietly dropped and now an electric fire provides part of the heat in The Queen's Drawing Room.

As with most of the Royal residences,

A view of the Drawing Room before the beautiful rugs from the Gulf States were received and before the piano was moved to the opposite side of the room on the orders of the Duke of Edinburgh. (Courtesy of the late Sir Hugh Janion)

the Yacht contains a number of items that have been given to the Royal Family over the years. Sitting on top of the piano in the Drawing Room is a gold rose bowl depicting the four castles belonging to Sultan Qabsso Bin Said and presented to The Queen in 1979.

The Lord High Admiral's Verge (rod of office) was made for the Duke of York in 1660 for use on State occasions, and when The Queen became Lord High Admiral in 1964, the Verge was presented to her by the Lord Commissioners of the Admiralty. It is carried annually at the Lord High Admiral's Divisions at Dartmouth, and preceded Her Majesty into dinner in *HMS Ark Royal* at the Spithead Review in Jubilee Year, 1977.

Over the fireplace hangs a picture by J. A. Wilcox. This depicts the scene at the Pool of London when The Queen returned from her first Commonwealth Tour as Sovereign in 1954, which was

also the first time she used the Yacht.

Arguably the most unique article of furniture is the gimbal table in the Drawing Room. Designed by Prince Albert, Consort to Queen Victoria, for her own Royal Yacht, *Victoria & Albert*, in the days long before stabilisers had been invented, it makes ingenious use of weights so that a gin and tonic can be safely left on its surface in almost any weather conditions up to and including a Force Eight gale without spilling a drop. At least that's the theory! No one among the present staff claims to have put it to the test in heavy weather.

Alongside the fireplace in one corner stands the television set. When *Britannia* is in port she receives whatever local stations are available; at sea they rely on videos for entertainment. At one time the television set rested on a distinctly 'un-Royal' stand. Then in 1987 when *Britannia* was at Plymouth for a major re-fit which included restoring much of her furniture and fittings, the craftsmen working in the Royal Apartments asked Lieutenant Commander Bob Henry, at that time Keeper and Steward, if The Queen would like them to make her a more suitable television cabinet.

This is the sort of decision that can only be taken at the highest level. Drawings were submitted to Buckingham Palace for Her Majesty's approval, which was given after several discussions with the Duke of Edinburgh, and the results can be seen today. The cabinet complements perfectly the older furniture in the Drawing Room, and the men who made it even managed to copy exactly the scalloped edges which are seen in other parts of the room. Looking at it today one would be hard pressed to believe that it is only circa 1987.

On top of the television cabinet is a gold epergne around which can be placed a complicated arrangement in which to place flowers, which is done only when the Royal Family is on board. A more recent arrival is a rather unusual looking little clock which stands on the desk. When The Queen launched *HMS Lancaster*, a Type 23 Frigate in 1991, she was presented with the clock as a memento and decided to give it a home in the Royal Yacht. The desk itself is satinwood and was used by Queen Victoria in the *Victoria & Albert II*.

The Drawing Room on *Britannia* is used in precisely the same way as the drawing rooms in any country house, for relaxing, conversation and games. The Royal Family has always enjoyed cards and there are several beautiful old card tables which are among the most frequently used items on board. When the adults are not playing bridge, whist or poker, the children commandeer them for Monopoly, Ludo and Snakes & Ladders – and there's usually a large jigsaw puzzle on the go whenever The Queen is embarked.

The decor in the Drawing Room is reflected throughout the Royal Apartments: white painted walls and ceilings, lustre bronze metalwork and dark mahogany woodwork. The Keeper and Steward of the Royal Apartments is able to ring the changes in the Drawing Room and ante-room as he keeps three sets of loose covers and curtains. The most popular colour scheme is one of green and white with a pattern of various birds. Another is in blue and white with a peacock motif, and the third is very pale, almost cream, which they use in the tropics. The curtains used with this set are gold with a tiny scroll embossed.

The Queen takes a personal interest in all the soft furnishings in the Royal Apartments. She chooses them herself, spending hours sorting through samples and pattern books. Nothing is ever thrown away. The covers are chosen to suit the occasion and the weather. The best, as far as their condition is concerned, are reserved for the most important visitors. But when the Yacht goes to the Western Isles on The Queen's annual summer cruise, no outside visitors are invited; it's just the Royal Family and the Household, so the older sets are used.

As the Keeper of the Royal Apartments says: 'When we're not on show to the world a little bit of commonsense goes into the housekeeping'.

Between the Drawing Room and the Dining Room, the other main State Apartment, are the foyer and the Grand Staircase which leads up to the bedroom suites of The Queen and the Duke of Edinburgh on the Shelter Deck. There are four bedrooms on this deck which are at the very top of the Yacht and when Prince Charles and the Princess Royal were small they used to have A and B suites alongside their parents' accommodation.

On the Main Deck, two decks below, are 16 cabins, each one with its own bathroom and lavatory. Cabin number 14 is the one favoured by most of the Royal Family on this deck. The Prince of Wales has used it and so has Prince Edward. It is a roomy cabin with round scuttles, and the curtains, soft furnishings and bedspread are all coloured gold which gives the room a warm, comfortable feeling. Cabin 9 is also highly regarded and the Princess Royal likes to use it when she is on board, as does the Duke of York. The colour scheme here is pale green so the room seems cooler than some of the others.

Members of the Household also have their favourite cabins which they always occupy when on board.

Sir Robert Fellowes, The Queen's Private Secretary, uses Cabin number 6 which is one of the largest of the Household cabins and has an adjoining office. His Deputy always occupies number 8. Opposite, in number 7, is The Queen's Surgeon. It's an efficient system as on each voyage there is no confusion about who sleeps where. Everyone knows where they are supposed to be and The Queen has a direct telephone line to each of her most senior aides' cabins. She also likes things to remain unchanged as far as possible so the orderly routine of life in any of the Royal residences is transferred without any fuss when they come on board *Britannia*.

If an important guest is staying overnight on the Yacht, Her Majesty will ensure their comfort by giving them the Guest Suite, choosing suitable books for their bedside table and fresh flowers to decorate the suite. The Guest Suite consists of Cabins 9 and 11 which are joined by a sitting room. Number 9 is a twin-bedded cabin with en suite facilities, while 11 contains a large single bed and it also has its own bathroom and lavatory. This is converted into the Nursery Suite

The Grand Staircase leading down from the Shelter Deck where The Queen and the Duke of Edinburgh have their bedroom suites. (Courtesy H.M. Yacht)

when children are on board.

When other members of the Royal Family are embarked, the Master of the Household suggests where they will stay, but the accommodation plan for every trip is approved personally by The Queen if she is going to be on board. The problems arise when extra staff have to be brought along with members of the family. Because there is a limited number of cabins, when you go down to the lower decks where the staff live you find that one extra person on the higher levels has a 'domino' effect; everyone moves down one until at the very lower end of the scale a poor junior footman finds he's doubled up with another when he expected to enjoy a cabin to himself.

As in all Royal residences The Queen and Prince Philip have separate bedrooms. When the Yacht was being fitted out, great care was taken to ensure that each of them was given exactly what they wanted. For example, they both prefer blankets and sheets to duvets, but the dimensions of Her Majesty's bedclothes differ from those of His Royal Highness. This is because Her Majesty likes a deeper turnback.

To supplement the old sheets supplied from the *Victoria & Albert* The Queen ordered 18 sheets measuring 80-ins x 112-ins with four rows of drawn thread at the top and shire stitching at the foot. The sheets are embossed with a personal monogram 'HM The Queen' measuring exactly 3$\frac{1}{2}$-ins. There was a certain amount of correspondence between the contractors and Buckingham Palace before the final size and style of the monogram was approved by Her Majesty, and several drawings were submitted for her consideration.

The same thing happened with the pillow cases. They had to measure 22-ins x 29-ins, be made of linen cambric with a lace border and the monogram is a more discreet 1$\frac{1}{2}$-ins high. The sheets cost £13.7.6 each and the pillow cases £6.12.6 each. The Duke of Edinburgh's sheets are slightly smaller than The Queen's: 80-ins x 108-ins, so they cost a little less: £12.19.6 each. His pillows are the same size but without the lace borders (on his own explicit instructions) and they cost £5.14.6 each. Like The Queen he has a dozen pillow cases.

The bed linen was supplied by Walpole Brothers of Sloane Street, London, who are able to boast that they have supplied bed linen for three reigns. The total cost for equipping the Royal bedrooms in 1952 was £498.12.0 but this amount included 170 sheets, 64 pillow cases and 50 bolsters for the Royal Household cabins on board the yacht.

The Dining Room is the State Apartment used for the truly grand occasions. It also doubles as a cinema when on Royal duty, and on Sundays it is used for church services. Unlike most ships of her size *Britannia* does not carry her own chaplain and this has led in the past to a number of disagreements between The Queen and her Lords of the Admiralty.

In the latter part of 1952 and early in 1953, shortly after the launching of *Britannia*, the Chaplain of the Fleet, the Navy's senior clergyman, wrote to the Second Sea Lord, urging that a permanent chaplain should be appointed to the crew of the Royal Yacht. In his letter he said: 'If no chaplain is borne, the impression would be given that . . . religious ministrations are a matter of indifference . . . and no communion would be available'. This was a question that could only be decided by The Queen herself. The then Flag Officer Royal Yachts, Vice-Admiral Abel-

The State Dining Room can seat 56 people in comfort which is the usual number invited when The Queen holds a formal dinner on board. The table decoration on the right of the picture is of two solid gold camels and was a gift from the Ruler of Dubai. (Courtesy H.M. Yacht)

Smith, was asked to convey the request to Her Majesty.

It was thought to be merely a formality that would be immediately approved. However, The Queen reacted in a way that was slightly surprising from the Defender of the Faith, and on 20 October 1953 Admiral Abel-Smith wrote to the Secretary of the Admiralty saying, 'The Queen does not see the need for a permanent chaplain on board. If a Church of England chaplain was required he could be obtained from one of the escorting ships'. And that was the end of the matter. *Britannia* does not have a chaplain to this day.

Sunday services are taken by the Commodore and it is the only occasion when all ranks are permitted to enter the Dining Room. The service is inter-

denominational and never varies. Three hymns, a short address and a reading from the Bible, all of which is usually over in less than 15 minutes.

The Dining Room is undoubtedly grand. The panelling and ceiling are white with gold trim, and the floor is carpeted throughout with the two-tone silver grey which runs through from the Drawing Room.

The large dining table is mahogany, and fully extended it seats 32 people in comfort. Running down the centre of the table is an electric pad several inches wide, the whole length and breadth of which is live. This means that the candelabras used to illuminate the table (which are all electric, not conventional candles) can be plugged in at any point. The base of each candelabra has the

usual three-point pins and these simply connect with any part of the electric pad, making the decoration and configuration of the table easy to change if necessary. It is an invention that is claimed to be unique to the Royal Yacht and the credit for its introduction is given to the late Earl Mountbatten of Burma.

The dining table itself is made in five sections. Any of these can be removed to make it smaller for family meals, while for a full-scale State Banquet the seating capacity can be increased to 56 by adding two extending tables which came from the *Victoria & Albert III.*

It was Prince Philip who solved the problem of how to increase the seating capacity in the Dining Room. When the Yacht was first commissioned he realised that the table they had bought was too small for the sort of State functions that would be held. To prove his point he brought a number of the staff from Buckingham Palace to the Yacht and ordered the chefs to prepare a full-scale banquet. They used the same table settings, china, plate and cutlery that would be used for formal banquets with The Queen present, and His Royal Highness soon discovered that the maximum number they could cope with, even with a couple of extra chairs squeezed in, was 32.

It was as a result of his experiment that the two extending tables were added, bringing the seating capacity up to its present strength of 56. Even this figure presents problems on occasions. Up to a third of those invited to State Banquets are usually members of the Royal Household or senior officers serving in the Royal Yacht, so there are not all that many invitations available to

The Dining Room seen from the opposite end. The chairs are of Hepplewhite design, but they are not all original. Some came from previous Royal Yachts while the remainder are copies. (Courtesy of the late Sir Hugh Janion)

outside guests. Of course one of the great advantages of having a comparatively small number is that they all get to meet The Queen, and she is able to devote much more time to them than she would if the function were being held ashore where the guest lists run to hundreds. This is just one of the reasons why an invitation to dine on board *Britannia* is so highly prized.

GIVEN STRING OF FEATHER MONEY

The dining chairs are in the Hepplewhite style, but not all are original. Some are Victorian, having been brought from the *Victoria & Albert*, while the remainder are modern copies, indistinguishable from the older items. Also brought from the previous Royal Yacht were the four 19th century sideboards carved in the style of Chippendale. On the after bulkhead is an oil painting by Atkin, of the *Victoria & Albert II* on a visit to Cork with Queen Victoria embarked.

Many of the objects adorning the walls of the Dining Room are mementoes of countries visited by *Britannia* during her 42-year lifetime. There is a whale rib bone collected by Prince Philip from a beach at Deception Island in 1957, a sword dated 1738 which was presented to The Queen by the Royal Swedish Navy in 1956, and a Narwhal tusk, a gift from Prime Minister Trudeau of Canada, in the North West

Territories in 1970. On either side of the entrance doors are two ceremonial swords and daggers presented to the Duke of Edinburgh in the Gulf States in 1979. He was also given a string of feather money in Santa Cruz in 1957. At the time it was worth around £15.

The centre alcoves in the room contain two of the most impressive items. They are silver gilt vases known as the Nelson and Collingwood Cups and commemorate the victory of the British Fleet over those of France and Spain at Trafalgar on 21 October 1805. They were presented to the families of Admiral Nelson and Lord Collingwood by the Patriotic Fund on behalf of the nation and subsequently purchased for King Edward VII. One was found in a public sale room, the other was bought privately from a watchmaker in Portsea.

Elsewhere in the recessed alcoves around the walls are arrows and boomerangs from Woomera, Australia, 1956; a pine wood plaque from Norfolk Island, 1974; a conch shell picked up during the Caribbean cruise of 1966; a mallet and fighting club from Tonga, 1970; a ceremonial pig killer from the New Hebrides tour in 1971; a Maori Chief's truncheon, called a mere, from Wanganui, New Zealand, 1954.

There is a Mother of Pearl necklace given to The Queen in Tuvalu in 1982, a carved Tosakanth engraved with glass beads, a reminder of a trip to Bangkok in 1972, and a wooden carving of a shark signed by all the adults living on Pitcairn Island in 1971. A stone figure and a carved wooden tortoise were gifts from Easter Island in 1971, and a ceremonial dagger was presented to Prince Philip by the Wali of Niza in Eastern Arabia in 1979. The visit to Raratonga in 1971 provided the wooden figure in the first alcove on the port side. In the second alcove are silver, gold and ivory

After a refit in 1970, the hammocks were done away with and replaced by conventional bunks, but one man, Leading Seaman Jamie Stewart, who had never used an ordinary bed, was given special permission to keep his hammock.

daggers from Malaysia, 1972, and a Sioux peace pipe from the American Plains, given during the State Visit to the United States in July 1976 as part of the Bicentennial Celebrations.

Steel drums from Trinidad are souvenirs of the 1966 Caribbean cruise, while a whale tooth was received in Fiji in 1970. One of the earliest voyages of *Britannia* is remembered by the slate daggers from New Guinea in 1956. The sharks-teeth swords came from the Solomon Islands in 1959. Among all these ethnic offerings is the unlikely gift of a cricket bat and ball from Samoa in 1974. There are also a number of silver sailing boats mounted on stone, presented when *Britannia* visited Kingston

(Ontario) for the sailing events in the Montreal Olympic Games of 1976.

When guests sit down to a formal dinner on board, the principal decoration of the table is a very valuable sculpture of two gold camels under two palm trees. It was given to The Queen by the Ruler of Dubai during the State Visit to the Gulf States in 1979. It is said to be the most valuable single item in *Britannia*. However, the Keeper of the Royal Apartments, who knows the cost of every piece on board, says that the insurance values are never disclosed. Privately it has been revealed that the object is worth over £1 million. Nobody, apart from the donor perhaps, would describe the piece as handsome,

The Queen's sitting room or day cabin which is used by Her Majesty as an office when she is on board. This is where she works on her 'boxes' every day and where she gives private audiences. (Courtesy of the late Sir Hugh Janion)

but it does have a certain attraction, and it is definitely a talking point among those seeing it for the first time. There is a remarkable attention to detail in the piece, the craftsmen even placing bunches of tiny dates on the palm trees. Closer inspection reveals that the dates are rubies.

On the same deck as the State Apartments are the day cabins of The Queen and Prince Philip. Here again much use has been made of old furniture and fittings. In The Queen's sitting room the sofa and armchair were used in two previous Royal ships. The first occasion was in *HMS Vanguard* in 1946, and the second was in the *SS Gothic* for the Coronation Tour of 1953. The four wheatsheaf pattern panel light brackets, made of wood and painted in old silver, were also obtained from the *SS Gothic* where they were installed in The Queen's Drawing Room. As was the ornate mirror above the fireplace (the fireplace itself contains a small electric heater). There are a couple of water-colours in the sitting room. They are by Alan Linford and are of scenes of the River Thames, circa 1949. There is also a watercolour of *Britannia* by Sir Hugh Casson.

The sitting room is rarely used as such. It is more of an office. The Queen spends several hours there every day working on her papers. She has a desk and telephone console linking her

Prince Philip's sitting room. The main decoration is a scale model of HMS Magpie, *His Royal Highness's first naval command.* (Courtesy of the late Sir Hugh Janion)

directly with her Private Secretary's room and even though her Page is always on hand, there is no outer office to act as a filter; the sitting room leads directly off the main lobby. The Queen uses this room to give audiences and to discuss matters of State business with her Private Secretary.

Prince Philip's sitting room, which is exactly the same size as The Queen's but on the opposite side of the Yacht, is also functional rather than luxurious. While he also enjoys Alan Linford's water-colours his main decoration is a scale model of *HMS Magpie*, his first naval command in 1950 in the rank of Lieutenant Commander. (The Duke of Edinburgh holds the rank of Admiral of the Fleet, the only rank in the Royal Navy in which the holders never 'retire'; they move on to 'half-pay' but officially remain for life on the Navy List.) Prince Philip's day cabin, which he calls his study, is where he works with his Private Secretary. It is conveniently situated if he wants to have a private conversation with any of the guests on board.

The main difference between the State Apartments on *Britannia* and those at Buckingham Palace or Windsor Castle, apart from the size of course, is that ashore, the Apartments are rarely used except for formal occasions. On board, they are very much a part of the everyday life of the Royal Family.

Although they lack nothing in splendour, there is a homeliness about them that helps make visitors feel comfortable. The Queen and her family use the Drawing Room and State Dining Room every day, even if there are only around half a dozen or so for dinner. They never seem lost because the rooms are not that large. It is quite easy to see why The Queen refers to *Britannia* as 'my home afloat'.

BRITANNIA ENTERTAINS

D RESS AT A formal function on board *Britannia* depends on the climate. In the tropics evening wear is a thin dinner jacket with decorations for civilians. Naval officers wear white mess dress: black trousers, short white 'monkey' jacket, and black tie. Ladies always wear full length evening dresses and The Queen and other ladies in the Royal Family wear tiaras.

At sea, life is a little less formal. There is an outfit for officers known as Red Sea Rig which consists of black trousers, cummerbund and an open-neck shirt. This is worn only when there are no official guests. The Queen enjoys the informality of Red Sea Rig and when this is worn she too will 'dress down', perhaps in a sleeveless knee-length dress with the minimum of jewellery.

Although life on board is naturally less formal than at one of the palaces ashore, there is no reduction in the standard of service, dress or behaviour. Footmen and Naval Stewards wear livery at State Banquets, while the china and cutlery are from King Edward VII's

Prime Ministers, Presidents and Potentates all enjoy being invited to a function on Britannia. *Here President Gerald Ford and his wife are entertained by The Queen who is the nation's hostess.* (David Secombe)

The occasion is one of the Commonwealth Prime Ministers Conferences when The Queen gives a reception and State Banquet on board. Here she is with Rajiv Ghandi, then Prime Minister of India, Mrs (now Baroness) Thatcher, and Mr Mulroney, Canada's Prime Minister. (Terry Fincher)

reign. The food is prepared and cooked by Buckingham Palace chefs who are ably assisted by Navy Chief Cook 'Swampy' Marsh, working alongside them in the Royal Galley.

The equipment is very functional. It works perfectly most of the time, but some of it is 42 years old and requires constant attention. For example, most of the electrical items are all driven by direct current instead of the more modern alternating current. As replacements for such items are virtually impossible to find, if anything breaks down it has to be repaired on the spot. There's a considerable amount of ingenuity to be

When the tables are being laid, as much attention to detail is paid as there is when the function is being held at Buckingham Palace. A Banquet afloat is a truly spectacular occasion. (David Secombe)

found in the electrical department. Another problem for the Royal chefs is that they have to learn to work in conditions which are cramped to say the least. At Buckingham Palace the kitchens are vast. On board *Britannia* the very opposite pertains, and this is where the naval cooks' experience comes into its own. They are well used to working in confined areas.

A State Banquet on *Britannia* is a truly magnificent occasion, no less auspicious for being held in a room a tenth of the size of the State Ballroom at

The Keeper and Steward of the Royal Apartments checks every place setting with a ruler to ensure that each one is exactly the same distance from its neighbour. (Courtesy H.M. Yacht)

The food eaten by the Royal Family and that used for State Banquets is brought from Buckingham Palace. Many of the flowers come from the gardens at Windsor Castle. (Courtesy H.M. Yacht)

Buckingham Palace. The attention to detail, a byword in Royal service, leaves nothing to be desired.

When the tables at Buckingham Palace are being laid, the Palace Steward checks the position of each place setting with a ruler; the Keeper and Steward of the Royal Apartments does the same thing on board the Royal Yacht. He supervises the laying of the Royal table, making sure the five Brierly crystal glasses – two for wine, one each for champagne, water and port, and all bearing the Royal cypher EIIR – are placed in precisely the correct order, and that the place names and menus, printed prior to *Britannia* sailing, and brought on board with the rest of the stores, are all as they should be.

The Master of the Household is responsible for arranging, with The Queen's approval, the seating plan. He pays particular attention to titles and decorations on the place settings. The menus are in French, illustrated with a picture of the Yacht, and these are given

to the guests as souvenirs when they leave.

The crystal and precious china is all washed by hand. Very few breakages have been recorded. Members of the crew volunteer to do the washing up after a banquet – the gentlest hands are said to belong to the stokers.

The Royal supplies of food are carefully loaded into *Britannia* at Portsmouth wherever possible, prior to sailing. Items such as fresh fruit and salad vegetables are bought locally, subject to quality and availability. The wine

The Princess spent most of the days in her bikini. If she decided she wanted to go 'walk-about' through the rest of the yacht she would slip a simple summer skirt over her swimsuit. She enjoyed exploring Britannia's *lower decks. The crew soon became used to the sight of her peering into cupboards and cabins, messdecks and galleys.*

H.M.Y. BRITANNIA

MENU

Couronne de Homard Canadienne

Suprême de Pintade Farcie
aux Airelles Rouges
Choux de Bruxelles Nouveaux
Courgettes Forestière
Pommes Fines Herbes

Salade

Andrassy Pudding

LES VINS
Pokolbin Chardonnay 1989
Château Labégorce-Zédé 1982
Graham 1963

MERCREDI LE 12 DECEMBRE 1990   POOL OF L

Menus are printed in French and when The Queen is present they are illustrated with a picture of the Yacht. These are then given to guests as they leave as mementoes of the occasion.

SAUMON FUME

SELLE D'AGNEAU SARLADAISE

SALADE

GLACE VANILLE
SAUCE BUTTERSCOTCH

JEUDI LE 15 AOUT 1991

When the Royal Family is not embarked, the menus in the Ward Room are printed on plain white cards with the Royal Cypher at the head.

Creme Cressoniere

****

Supreme de Grouse
fines herbes

Haricots Verts

Courgettes

Pommes Nouvelles

Salade

****

Bombe aux Prunes

HMY Britannia   lundi
at Kingston   le 28 octobre

On this occasion, Prince Charles was the senior Royal on board, in Kingston, Jamaica, so the emblem of the Prince of Wales was used to decorate the menu.

served at table comes from *Britannia's* own cellar. This is stocked by the Royal Warrant holder for the Yacht, John Harvey & Sons of Bristol.

The Master of the Household has the ultimate responsibility for the service of food and administration of Royal events. He is assisted by Michael Jephson, his Chief Clerk, and the Catering Manager.

To ensure the highest standards are maintained on board, the Page of the Presence, The Queen's Page and the Naval Chief Steward supervise the serving of the food and wines. They form a very experienced team. With their eyes everywhere, missing nothing, they strive constantly for that peak of perfection known on the Royal Yacht as 'unobtrusive excellence'.

There is a refrigerated store on board in which fresh flowers are kept. Often these have been brought from the Royal Gardens at Windsor, but the Steward who arranges them in the Royal Apartments also buys local flowers in the countries visited.

A staff of 14 Naval stewards work exclusively in the Royal Apartments.

One of the most delicate tasks after every function is the washing up, and the cleaning of the silver. This is all done by hand and so far there have been very few breakages and nothing has ever gone missing! (Courtesy H.M. Yacht)

They operate in tandem with the Pages and Footmen from Buckingham Palace who always accompany The Queen when she comes on board. Then, the service of food in the Dining Room becomes the responsibility of the Keeper and Steward of the Royal Apartments.

One of the first things to happen when the principal guests arrive on *Britannia* is that the official photographs are taken by 'Snaps' – the Yacht's photographer, Dave Hunt. These are then rushed into processing and developed and printed during the meal. The Queen is shown them discreetly and she chooses which ones she prefers, which are quietly signed by her and Prince Philip. Once this has been completed the pictures are framed so that Her Majesty can present them to her guests as a memento of the evening before they leave.

When The Queen and her guests have taken their places at dinner the Dining Room doors are closed. This allows the Royal Marines orchestra to set up in the ante-room with maximum speed and minimum noise. When the Director of Music is ready, the Dining Room doors are re-opened and The Queen and her guests enjoy a programme of suitable music throughout the meal. The orchestra have to 'disappear' before Her Majesty and guests re-enter the ante-room at the end of the banquet.

PRESSES BUZZER FOR NEXT COURSE

At Buckingham Palace and Windsor Castle there is a system of 'traffic lights' installed in the State Dining Rooms so that the footmen can be summoned when they are needed to clear away dishes and serve the next course. On board *Britannia*, Prince Philip has a

One of the more distinctive characteristics of Britannia *is the single gold line painted around her hull. The paint really is gold leaf and the original cost was £332. This has since escalated as the line has to be repainted every time the yacht has a refit.*

buzzer near his hand for the same purpose. When he's ready for the next part of the meal he presses the buzzer and the staff, who are waiting outside the door, come in.

Things don't often go wrong at official functions on board. But there is the occasional hiccup, as happened when President Ronald Reagan was invited to dinner on *Britannia* during The Queen's visit to the United States in 1991. A BBC television crew was filming the event as part of a documentary programme to mark the 40th anniversary of Her Majesty's accession in 1992.

When the guests were taking coffee in the Drawing Room after dinner, the viewers all saw Mrs Reagan making a great fuss about President Reagan having decaffeinated coffee. Lieutenant Commander Bob Henry, who was Keeper and Steward of the Royal Apartments at the time, knows the real story. 'It was towards the end of the meal when my Petty Officer was going around the table offering Port. He asked the President, "Would you like some Port?" But the President, who is hard of hearing, thought he was being offered coffee and he replied, "I don't mind as long as it's decaffeinated". Well, we had never heard of decaffeinated Port, of course, and The Queen, who was sitting next to the President, thought it was quite amusing. So when they all went through into the Drawing Room for their coffee and liqueurs she made sure

Royal Yachtsmen are easily identified ashore when they are in civilian clothes. Even in the hottest climates they are required to wear collars and ties after 6.30 p.m.

that, at last, he got his decaffeinated coffee.' Everyone was happy and *Britannia's* reputation for giving exemplary service was maintained without a blemish.

Royal servants are trained to keep a straight face no matter what happens. In 1971, Prince Philip had taken over *Britannia* for a tour that included the Galapagos Islands. At one of the ports of call he gave a dinner on board for 36 guests including the Islands' Minister of Defence, who had brought an Ecuadorian friend with him. As one of the footmen unfolded the linen table

napkin and placed it on the lap of this guest, he picked it up and promptly blew his nose in it. The footman's face was a study as all the other guests politely ignored the gesture.

The food served is excellent without being ostentatious. A typical menu for a State Banquet was that served on 29 May 1992 in Valletta for the President of Malta and Mrs Tabonne. Just before the meal The Queen had given the President and his wife a number of gifts including a pair of photographs of herself and Prince Philip in silver frames, a 19th century clock and case engraved with ER and PP cyphers, and a Baccarat Vase, also engraved EIIR.

It was a three-course dinner. The starter was Terrine of Sole and Salmon, followed by a main course of Fillet of Roast Veal cooked in mushrooms, with

Prince Philip is watched by his uncle, Earl Mountbatten of Burma, as he receives a gift from the local headman during Britannia's *visit to Fiji and the Galapagos Islands. (Courtesy of the Broadlands Archives)*

carrots, buttered asparagus and new potatoes, plus salad. Icecream is always a favourite and on this occasion The Queen and her guests were served a delicacy called Bombe Glacée Royale. Menus often include speciality dishes named with a particular Royal slant such as Scampi à la Windsor, Filet de Boeuf *Britannia*, or Compote d'Oranges Sandringham. These are simply dishes which have proved to be popular with the Royal Family at one of the Royal residences and are known by the place where they originated.

Grace is not said before dinner – or any other meal – and even though The Queen and her guest of honour exchange toasts, speeches are kept to a minimum. Smoking is not encouraged at the table, but Her Majesty has no objection to guests doing so in the Drawing Room either before or after dinner.

The function invariably ends with The Queen leading her guests on deck to watch one of the highlights of the evening, Beat Retreat by the Royal Marines on the quayside. These are the same musicians who played as an orchestra during the banquet. If the ceremony is performed after sunset it is still more spectacular under floodlights. Even though Her Majesty has seen it hundreds of times, and it rarely alters, she is said to get as much of a kick out of this as any of her guests seeing it for the first time.

The Queen and the Duke of Edinburgh say goodnight to their principal guests before they are escorted to the Royal gangway. There the Yacht's Senior Commander is in attendance to salute them and the other guests as they go ashore.

The Royal Marines Band is completely self-contained. They even carry their own floodlights for the occasions when they perform at night.

The author chatting with Commander Paul Jackson, at that time the Admiral's secretary, on the Verandah Deck. (Photograph by David Hunt)

During Beat Retreat, the Steward's team will have cleared the Dining Room and Drawing Room so that Her Majesty, His Royal Highness and members of the Household can have a nightcap before they retire. By the time they return to the Drawing Room it will have been restored to its original pristine condition with little sign of the party that had gone on earlier.

Evening functions are usually over by midnight. But it is sometimes well after that hour before every item of silver, china and glassware has been cleaned, polished, accounted for and returned to its rightful place until the next time. Then, and only then, do the senior staff settle back with a glass of something of a distinguished vintage, to review the events of the day in their own minds, and to see if there is any way in which the occasion could have been improved. This is why *Britannia* is so envied throughout the world. They are never satisfied, never complacent, always looking to do better next time.

THE HOUSEHOLD

BRITANNIA TAKES ON an added dimension when Royalty are embarked, particularly if The Queen and the Duke of Edinburgh are on board.

For a State Visit, Her Majesty will be accompanied by an entourage of at least 45. These range from her personal staff: Private Secretaries (at least two always travel with her, the third remaining at Buckingham Palace 'minding the shop'), her Press Secretary, the Master of the Household who is responsible for all domestic matters when The Queen is on board, dressers, valets, chefs, footmen, chauffeurs, if the Rolls-Royce is being carried, police officers from the Royalty Protection Department, a hairdresser, surgeon (plus a bag of the Royal Family's homeopathic medicines), clerical and administration assistants, information officers and a whole host of others who have been brought from Buckingham Palace for the duration of the voyage, including several official government representatives. So it is not

Police officers and members of the Household of the Prince of Wales carefully supervise the loading of his luggage before a voyage. (Jayne Fincher)

When the Royal Household comes on board it can mean up to 45 extra people plus tons of additional baggage, which is all the responsibility of the Travelling Yeoman. (Photographers International)

too difficult to see the difference this many extra people make to life on the Royal Yacht.

Most of those accompanying The Queen are old hands. They know exactly what they have to do and where they are going to be living, so they move into their quarters, which have been allocated by the Master of the Household, after consulting with the Keeper of the Royal Apartments, quietly and effortlessly.

The Queen's Private Secretary, her doctor and the Master of the Household occupy the same cabins time after time, so too do the Press Secretary and the other senior members of the Household. This works in precisely the same way as when the Court moves from Buckingham Palace to any of the other Royal residences. There's no panic, little fuss, and work continues with the minimum disruption.

The Queen's 'Boxes' containing Government and other official papers are delivered each day no matter where Her Majesty is anywhere in the world. Immediately after breakfast her Private Secretary, Sir Robert Fellowes, joins her in her study where they go over the programme for the day and he brings any additional telegrams that may have arrived during the night that need Royal attention.

The Queen's paperwork usually takes up a couple of hours, even on the days when she is officially off duty. If they are in port or due to arrive at a new destination, a copy of the day's events will have been photographically reduced to a size convenient to fit into pockets and hand-

Years of Royal training had instilled in Prince Charles reservations about going where he was not expected, and he remained in the Royal Apartments throughout the honeymoon voyage. It simply would not have occurred to him to do otherwise.

bags, and everyone involved will be given one including Her Majesty.

The Press Secretary will deliver a summary of the previous day's media coverage and the Master of the Household brings a copy of the menus proposed for all meals that day. The menus for the formal occasions have

Wherever Britannia arrives she is greeted with pomp and ceremony. Here the colourfully dressed locals in Dominica watch as the bandmaster prepares for the Royal Salute. (Photographers International)

The Queen and the Duke of Edinburgh with members of the Royal Household on the quayside in San Diego during the State Visit to the west coast of the United States. (Photographers International)

Every trip has its official moments. The Duke of Edinburgh coming ashore at Pitcairn Island to make a courtesy call. Members of his staff bring up the rear carrying gifts and papers with the details of his programme. (Courtesy of the Broadlands Archives)

been printed in England long before the voyage began and they rarely change, but The Queen personally approves the day-to-day menus which are then printed on board.

There have been the odd occasions when events do not go as planned, but none was as potentially disastrous as in 1974 when the Royal Yacht was carrying The Queen during a State Visit to Indonesia. Her Majesty intended to give a State Banquet on board *Britannia* for the President in Djakarta harbour. It had all been arranged in some detail many months before, and agreed to by the President's aides.

However, on the afternoon of the banquet the Indonesians argued that they did not wish to come because 'the ladies might feel sick on board ship'. When these fears were allayed they then said that there was a risk of sabotage to the party, and finally claimed that *Britannia*

was too small for the size of the party they wanted to bring. It was pointed out to them that more people could be accommodated in comfort than at the British Embassy ashore and that the seating plan and numbers had all been worked out at the 'recce' visit months earlier. Eventually the real reason for their reluctance emerged. They admitted that 'We don't want the President travelling down in this dock area at night'.

So The Queen, who could do little else, agreed to change the venue of the Banquet. The Master of the Household had just a couple of hours to move the stewards, pages, footmen, cutlery, china, silver plate, wine and food, several miles to the British Embassy. That he managed to do all this and mount a magnificent banquet, even if the 50 odd guests had to sit at small round tables, was a tribute to his skill and the superb team work of the combined *Britannia* and Buckingham Palace staff.

Happily, this was a rare occurrence and one the Master – and The Queen – are not anxious to repeat.

MAY CHANGE FIVE TIMES A DAY

When The Queen is ashore carrying out official engagements, her staff on board settle into a daily routine. The dressers, working from a schedule they have been given earlier, press and lay out the out-fits Her Majesty will wear later that day. On a busy day The Queen can change clothes up to five times.

Prince Philip's valet organises his wardrobe, paying special attention to the decorations that will be worn during the visit. If he has been awarded an hon-our by the country they are visiting the valet will be extra careful about the con-dition of the decoration and the way it should be worn. At a State Banquet held in Malaysia, Prince Philip wore full evening dress, white tie and tails, plus

decorations. It was noticed that he was not wearing the Malaysian Order that The Queen was wearing. He explained that The Queen had declined to give the host Queen Consort an Order, and in retaliation, her husband had refused to give him one! If members of the Royal Family or the Household are offered honours by foreign countries they have to obtain the permission of The Queen before accepting.

The clerical staff work in their office on the deck just below the Household cabins, where the portable word proces-sors, filing cabinets and official station-ery are kept. The Keeper and Steward of the Royal Apartments checks that his team are preparing the Verandah Deck for The Queen's return (if she has gone ashore), and that the Royal cabins have been cleaned and dusted and any essen-tial repairs carried out.

The Queen and her family eat break-fast together in the Sun Lounge on the Verandah Deck, where they also take afternoon tea. They are usually joined by members of the Household for lunch

The Sun Lounge on the Verandah Deck is where The Queen and her family eat breakfast together, also afternoon tea. This room is strictly 'off-limits' to everyone else! (Courtesy of the late Sir Hugh Janion)

Preparations for the end of the voyage concert go on for days – and the end result gives wonderful entertainment to both cast and audience – Royal or otherwise!
(Courtesy of the Broadlands Archives)

and dinner in the Dining Room.

The Royal Marines Band rehearses in the morning and plays every evening during dinner. Their programme for official events has been chosen before leaving England, and also printed, so it is difficult to get anything changed. However, there is no advance programme for everyday informal occasions and the Director of Music has a free hand to vary the style and theme. He is generally happy to entertain requests, but if he is not sure about the music asked for he has a ready excuse, as the late Earl Mountbatten found out in 1972. *Britannia* was off the coast of Malaysia when one evening Lord Mountbatten asked for the theme from *The Tales of Beatrix Potter* (he wanted this particular piece because the film had been produced by his son-in-law, Lord Brabourne). He was told this would not be possible because all the music had

been selected and printed before the Yacht sailed and could not be altered.

When the Yacht is at sea, afternoons are for relaxing. Some members of the Household like to paint, take photographs or lie on their sunbeds and read. Whatever it is, they are usually free until tea time which is when the Yacht wakes up again.

Tea is taken in the Equerries Room. It is served by stewards and lasts about an hour. Then they all go back to work for a couple of hours before dressing for dinner. If there is an official function on board in the evening, the Household gathers in the ante-room to greet the guests. When they are all assembled The Queen and the Royal Family join them for introductions and a pre-dinner drink.

Britannia is also able to provide its own 'in house' brand of after dinner entertainment. Several of the Yachtsmen have worked up cabaret acts which they are delighted to perform in front of Royalty, and the more risqué the repertoire, the greater seems to be the Royal Family's enjoyment.

Towards the end of most cruises the crew and members of the Household stage a concert attended by the Royal Family. A lot of preparation goes into the show which usually makes up in enthusiasm what it may lack in quality. The performers take this quite seriously, making sure their make-up and costumes are perfect, and several rehearsals are held on the fo'c'sle before the big night.

During one cruise to New Zealand, The Queen and the Duke of Edinburgh sprang a surprise on the rest of the party when they suddenly decided to take part in the concert instead of just sitting in the audience as they usually do.

Lord Mountbatten took over the run-

ning of this particular show, (as, apparently, he always did whenever he was on board). It included The Queen's then Private Secretary, Sir Martin Charteris (now Lord Charteris of Amisfield), delivering a speech in impeccable Pidgin English.

Lord Mountbatten had schooled his cast in the words and actions of the Maori Haka, the traditional ceremonial greeting. The opening item on the programme was to be a re-enactment of the welcome given to The Queen when she stepped on to New Zealand soil for the first time – with someone else playing Her Majesty's part.

When the moment came for The Queen and Prince Philip to be shown to their seats, they walked instead straight on to the stage where they took part in a mock 'Official Arrival'. It caused a sensation. No-one in the 'cast' knew of the change in plan except Lord

When Lord Mountbatten was on board he always took over as producer and master of ceremonies; especially for the 'crossing the line ceremony'. Here he makes sure 'King' Neptune knows his lines. (Courtesy of the Broadlands Archives)

Mountbatten, and it turned out to be one of the most successful of the many ship's concerts that have been held on board *Britannia* – and the only time 'The Boss' has ever taken part!

To the outside world the image of the Royal Household is one of correctness at all times and rigid formality. It is sometimes hard to imagine the Lord Chamberlain or the Crown Equerry letting down their hair in front of the Royal Family, or making fools of themselves to amuse their colleagues.

But on board *Britannia* relaxing is

The original estimate for the new Royal Yacht amounted to £1,615,000 including £290,000 profit. Eventually, the final price was £2,098,000 – possibly the best bargain this century.

not only for The Queen and her family but, when the work is done, for everyone else too. When Lord Maclean was Lord Chamberlain, he and his wife would often be invited to join The

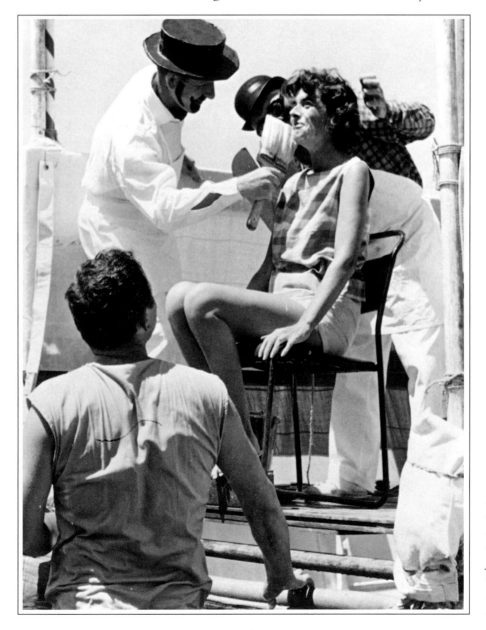

Lady Brabourne being 'given the treatment' as she crosses the Equator for the first time. (Courtesy of the Broadlands Archives)

When a Yachtsman meets one of the Royals he stands still until they have passed and speaks only if he has been acknowledged first, exactly the same system that applies throughout the Royal Household ashore.

Queen on their annual summer cruise to Scotland, and while Lady Maclean would sit quietly knitting on deck, Peter and Zara Phillips, the children of the Princess Royal, would dash around her chair playing games, or Prince Edward might even wind the wool for her. It was a purely domestic holiday scene which might take place anywhere; the only difference being that this was on board the most famous private yacht in the world and the Sovereign was sitting just a few feet away.

Britannia is always accompanied by an escort ship, sometimes more than one, whenever The Queen or the Prince of Wales are embarked. There was one occasion when the Yacht was temporarily abandoned by her escort at a most embarrassing moment for The Queen.

It was in the Indian Ocean and the frigate *HMS Arethusa* which was on escort duty, had left to answer an emergency call from the Maldive Islands. Just after it disappeared, three Russian submarines surfaced and came to have a closer look at *Britannia*. There was no danger, they were just curious, but The Queen was not terribly pleased that they should see the Royal Yacht sailing alone without any protection.

The weather of course, is no respecter of rank; neither are trade unions. The national dock strike of 1972 meant that in order to join the Yacht for her summer cruise, The Queen's train had to be diverted from Southampton (where The Queen boards) to Portsmouth and Her Majesty then had to be taken out to *Britannia*, waiting off Spithead, in the Royal Barge. When they eventually set sail the weather turned rough and as they rounded Land's End they ran headlong into a violent storm which kept both The Queen and Princess Anne confined to their beds until after lunchtime.

Britannia is a steady craft, fitted with stabilisers. But when the elements decide to play up there's very little she, or any other ship for that matter, can do about it.

Whenever The Queen or the Prince of Wales is on board, Britannia *is accompanied by an escort ship. This is the Royal Silver Jubilee Review of the Fleet at Spithead in 1977 with* HMS Birmingham *in close attendance.* (Courtesy of the Broadlands Archives)

The Royal Yacht cricket team plays matches against The Queen's Flight, Royal Protection Department and any opposition they can find on overseas tours.

When the Household is embarked they blend in with the officers and Yachtsmen as much as they can. The junior staff socialise with the Yachtsmen in the Unwinding Room, joining them for drinks and other

The NAAFI shop stocks everything from toothpaste to elegant crystal. Souvenirs bearing the Royal Yacht emblem are particularly popular. (Courtesy H.M. Yacht)

Cut glass whisky decanters at £58 have become collectors' items. So too have the champagne flutes and the tumblers, as these can only be bought on board Britannia.

activities that have been organised.

The NAAFI shop is open to everybody and is particularly popular with new members who like to buy the mementoes that are unique to the Royal Yacht. Cut glass whisky decanters at £58, tumblers and champagne glasses in presentation boxes, Wedgwood ashtrays and bon-bon dishes, T-shirts bearing the *Britannia* logo, a great favourite with the children and girl friends, pens, pencils, and *Britannia* headed writing paper. No male member of the Household would dream of leaving the Yacht without buying a *Britannia* tie, an exclusive souvenir that immediately marks you out as belonging to a very elite group.

One of the busiest members of the Household is the Travelling Yeoman. He looks after all the luggage of The Queen and the Palace staff. As this amounts to over five tons for every trip, his job is no sinecure. Not only does he make the travel arrangements for the Court and staff, both at home and

A wooden plaque bearing the Royal Coat of Arms and Britannia's cypher. It's the one souvenir everyone who has served on the Royal Yacht treasures.

abroad, he also assists in the Royal servery and makes sure that the correct newspapers and periodicals are distrib- uted to members of the Royal Family and Household wherever they are.

The officials of the Royal

The Ward Room, one of the most popular venues for members of the Royal Household, who love to be invited to join the Yacht's officers for an informal drink – or a more formal dinner. (Courtesy H.M. Yacht)

Divers accompany Britannia everywhere and regularly search beneath the Yacht, checking her condition and also for security reasons.

Household have their own mess and dining room, and they are also frequently invited to join the Yacht's officers in the Ward Room. These invitations are highly prized as *Britannia*'s officers are among the most hospitable in the Royal Navy and the atmosphere in the Ward Room is always jolly, informal and amusing. Nobody stands on ceremony. While guests are always treated most courteously, once they get to know you they regard you as an old friend, and this is why members of the Royal Household feel so welcome.

At the end of his first voyage on the Royal Yacht a former Press Secretary to The Queen remarked, 'I've never enjoyed the sea and the idea of having to work and live afloat didn't appeal to me one little bit. Now, I just can't wait for the next time'.

AT SEA

WHEN A STATE Visit by The Queen is being planned, a large number of things obviously have to be taken into consideration. These include the type of visit and the reason behind it: is it a reciprocal event in return for an incoming visit by a foreign Head of State (which is usually the case), a 'selling' trip organised by the Foreign Office to promote British exports, or simply a visit arranged because Her Majesty has never been to that particular country before?

Throughout her entire reign, it was not until June 1989 that The Queen made her first, and so far only, visit to Spain. She had long enjoyed a close personal friendship with King Juan Carlos and Queen Sofia, but the question of the position of Gibraltar had been a matter of some sensitivity for decades. Neither government would agree to their Royal Families exchanging visits until King Juan Carlos came to Britain for his first official visit in 1987. It was felt that if The Queen then returned the visit it would greatly improve relations between the two countries and after discussions over several years the date was finally set for June 1989.

Captain Peter Voute RN (now retired) was the Naval Attaché at the British Embassy in Madrid at the time. As soon as it had been decided that the Royal Yacht was to be used for the visit he became involved in making all the preliminary arrangements – and then seeing the visit through to its conclusion.

The State Visit was slightly longer than most. It lasted five days, Monday to Friday, with a weekend added on in Majorca where The Queen and the Duke of Edinburgh were to spend Saturday and Sunday with the King at his Summer Palace, while using the Yacht as a base.

The Royal Yacht was to be in Barcelona for The Queen's use after she had arrived in an aircraft of The Queen's Flight (Her Majesty always flies to her destination and the Yacht is there to meet her, thus saving time). On the Friday the Yacht would sail overnight to Palma where she would be berthed alongside in one of the most beautiful harbours in the world. All fairly simple and straightforward but, as with every-

> *When* **Britannia** *is in port, even when there is no member of the Royal Family on board, the officers dine in black tie; the best silver, china and cutlery are used and every dinner takes on a feeling of being a special occasion.*

Wherever she is in the world the mail follows Britannia. *Sacks of official documents for The Queen's attention are loaded by Yachtsmen to be sorted in the floating post office.* (Photographers International)

thing involving Royalty, it would mean scores of letters, signals and telephone calls between the Naval Attaché, *Britannia*, Buckingham Palace and the host country.

Nine months before the visit was scheduled, Captain Voute had his first letter from the Admiral then commanding *Britannia*. This informed him officially that the visit was to take place, and attached eight annexes listing the requirements of the Yacht.

The first annex gives the full list of points on which information is required, and the second is on navigation and berthing, together with three additional appendices giving a berthing diagram and brow arrangements (angle of gang plank). For example, the slope of the Royal Brow must not exceed 10 degrees at the times of embarkation or disembarkation of members of the Royal

At the start of the annual Western Isles cruise, The Queen is joined on this occasion by her youngest son, Prince Edward. (Photographers International)

Family, dinner and reception guests or officials making calls on members of the Royal Family. And no member of the Royal Family must be expected to step up or down more than eight inches when getting on or off the Yacht.

Another important point included in the information pack is that the Royal Yacht, when flying a Royal Standard is never led into harbour. The only occa-

The Queen is joined by the Duke of Edinburgh as they embark at Palermo. (Courtesy H.M. Yacht)

Britannia *receiving the customary 'fire hose' welcome as she enters Toronto harbour in 1991, dwarfed by the gigantic CN Tower, Canada's highest building. (Courtesy H.M. Yacht)*

sional exceptions to this rule are in the United Kingdom where Trinity House and Northern Lighthouse Board are allowed to exercise an ancient privilege.

Where small craft or aquatic welcomes are planned, it is important that measures are taken to keep participants clear of *Britannia*'s route. They should never cross ahead of the Yacht or her escort, and must be kept at least 20 degrees either side of the bow. Police control boats are needed but they must not use sirens unless absolutely necessary and never before nine o'clock in the morning.

Two tugs are needed to stand by only, when berthing alongside or at anchor, and when leaving. However well fendered, tugs will damage the ship's side paintwork if they push the Yacht or come alongside, and in consequence they should only do this in an emergency. The high gloss of *Britannia*'s paintwork has to be protected at all times. Two catamaran fenders are therefore normally required – a diagram is attached showing the correct dimensions and where they are to be positioned.

A separate annex gives details of how the Yacht's gangways are to be used:

Gangways – When the Royal Yacht is at anchor, or secured to a buoy, the gangways are used as follows:

Starboard after – The Royal Family, Heads of State and Queen's representatives of the equivalent rank of Governor and above.

Port after – Royal guests, Members of

The Hong Kong waterfront is the spectacular backdrop to Britannia. *The colony is one of the most popular destinations for the officers and crew.* (Photographers International)

The Princess Royal with her children, Zara and Peter Phillips, joining the Yacht for Cowes Week on the Isle of Wight. Britannia *is the focus of attention for many of the world's leading yachtsmen during the regatta.* (Courtesy H.M. Yacht)

the Household and visitors to the Royal Family.
Starboard Forward – Officers and Household Officials.
Port Forward – Royal Yachtsmen, Household Staff and all others.

Captain Voute was given a massive pack of instructions. He then had to liaise with his opposite numbers in the ports of Barcelona and Palma de Majorca, the Base Port Commanders, who were both Captains in the Spanish Navy. They included the Port Authorities in the initial discussions as both ports are civil administrations. He also had to employ the services of an agent who would be responsible for many details including fuel, provisions, foreign currency, and installing telephone lines (for the Barcelona visit 24 lines were needed).

The agent had to provide copies of local telephone directories and a list of useful numbers, together with English speaking operators to man *Britannia*'s exchange for the duration of the visit. The telephone bills were to be sent to *Britannia* immediately the visit was over with a print out of all calls so that the ship's accountant could identify private and Service calls. A further requirement was the loan of a police radio so that contact could be maintained with the Royal party whenever they were ashore.

The agent was given annex F which told him, among other things, that he was to provide:

Bread – White sliced wrapped.
Bread – Wholemeal sliced wrapped.
Milk – Fresh (long-life is acceptable if fresh is unavailable).

The bread and milk was to be delivered in non-returnable rigid cardboard containers and the invoices for the provi-

When Britannia anchored in secluded bays the Princess of Wales would swim alone at the stern of the Yacht while the staff and crew used the other end. Prince Charles rarely ventured into the sea, although he is a strong swimmer and enthusiastic wind-surfer, preferring to stay on deck sunbathing.

sions were to be sent to 'The Supply Officer, HM Yacht, *Britannia*'.

The next person to become involved was the Yacht's Liaison Officer who travelled to Barcelona and Palma to carry out the 'recce'. This is a separate preliminary visit from that made by The Queen's Private Secretary and her personal police officer before any Royal visit. They have to go over every step of the proposed itinerary, stop watches in hand, to check the times and distances between every segment of the programme. The Liaison Officer looked at exactly where *Britannia* was going to be berthed in both ports. He measured the dimensions of the landing stages, checked the water levels at times of landing and embarking, and examined the facilities for the bowman and stern-sheetman on the Royal Barge to hold on to with their boat-hooks.

One of the advantages for this visit was the fact that the Mediterranean is non-tidal so there was no problem with the rise and fall of the water.

POLICE BOAT MUST NOT ROCK BARGE

The Flag Officer Royal Yachts went to what might seem quite extraordinary lengths to avoid the highly polished side of *Britannia* coming into contact with stone jetties. Captain Voute discovered that Spanish fendering was by means of chains and enormous rubber tyres placed right at the bottom of the jetty. This would be no use to *Britannia* if she rolled with the wash of passing ships. What was needed was for the fenders to be lifted just three feet. But bureaucracy being what it is – in any country – this wasn't as simple as it sounds. In the end, as Captain Voute explained, 'Money changed hands and even then I had to personally supervise the workmen who were actually lifting the fenders and we didn't manage to finish the job until the day before the Yacht arrived'.

Another of the instruction annexes details what happens when The Queen uses the Royal Barge to get between the Yacht and the landing stage. The dimensions of the Royal Barge are given:

Length – 41-ft (12.5m)
Draught – 3-ft (0.9m)
Height of cabin above waterline – 3-ft 10-ins (1.17m)
Distance from bows to forward point of cabin step – 24-ft (7.3m)
Overall height from waterline – 8-ft 4-ins (2.54m)
Normal passage speed – 18 knots

There then follows instructions about *escort boats*:

When Her Majesty is embarked in the Royal Barge, a motor boat from *Britannia* is always in attendance as an escort and no other boat should attempt to provide an escort. However, if a police boat is used to clear the way ahead of pleasure boats it is important that the police boat is capable of matching the maximum speed of the Royal Barge (20 knots) and that the helmsman pays particular attention to ensure that the stern wash of his boat does not

The Royal Barge is always followed by a motor boat from Britannia. Any police launches which might precede the Barge must be capable of matching her speed of 20 knots. (Courtesy H.M. Yacht)

inconvenience the Royal Barge.

Annex D contains information about the ceremonial involved when *Britannia* arrives in a foreign port.

Salutes: Gun salutes are fired only by the Royal Squadron when *Britannia* is wearing a Royal Standard. As the Yacht is not fitted with saluting guns, salutes are normally fired by the Royal Escort. The normal procedure is for national salutes (21 guns) to be exchanged, the Royal Escort firing first followed by the host country's reply from either ashore or afloat. The national salutes are immediately followed by a Royal Salute (fired by the host country) which is not returned, making a total of 63 guns in all. It is essential that the Yacht is informed as early as possible of the host country's intentions for firing salutes so that proposals can be submitted for approval by The Queen.

A splendid view of Britannia, *dressed overall, as she waits for the Duke of Edinburgh to embark during Cowes Week.*

Dressing Ship Overall: *Britannia* and any escorts dress overall from the time of berthing until sunset (or time of departure) whenever members of the Royal Family are embarked, but it would be helpful if details could be forwarded of any local anniversaries or ceremonies for which it would be appropriate to dress ship when Royalty are not embarked.

Illuminating Ship: It is customary for the Royal Yacht and her escort to be floodlit each night from 30 minutes after sunset until two o'clock in the morning.

The information pack continues with the news that the Royal Yacht Band will play while *Britannia* is entering harbour and securing alongside, also from approximately five minutes before leaving until *Britannia* is well clear of the berth. It goes on to state that advance warning should be given if it is intend-ed that a local band should also perform on the jetty (on odd occasions it has been known for competing bands to try and outblow each other). The Royal Marines Band normally performs the ceremony of Beat Retreat alongside the Yacht after a reception. An area of 100 square feet (30m square) is needed but the Yacht provides its own floodlights, flagstaffs and spot lights.

It is customary for a ceremonial sentry to be provided by the local armed services or police if they so wish. Otherwise the Yacht provides its own. An appendix to this annex lists the duties and uniform to be worn by the sentry. When Royalty are embarked he will be dressed and equipped as a Ceremonial Sentry – Naval Dress No 1 (Winter) or No 6 (Tropical) with white webbing belt and anklets – and will be posted from just before morning colours until after the last guest of Royalty has left the Yacht or until the last member of the Royal Family has returned on board, whichever is the later.

When the Yacht is at anchor or at a buoy, a guard boat must be provided to patrol around her day and night while a Standard is flying. The guard boat should operate at a distance of 50-yds to prevent all craft and swimmers from approaching the Royal Yacht. The sea bed under the Yacht's berth and the adjacent area of the jetty must be searched by divers in the 24 hours preceding arrival.

For the duration of the visit a daily search dive should take place under the supervision of the Yacht's Diving Officer but should be as discreet as possible. The water police or host navy should maintain a continuous presence outboard of the Yacht with moving boat patrols. Guests for receptions on board should be vetted by Consular/Embassy staff on the jetty. All items for delivery

These sea birds found an unusual perch near the main mast, obviously completely unaware that they were sharing their temporary home with Royalty.

on board are scanned by an X-ray machine which is carried by the Yacht, and then sited near the berth in the foreign port.

The regulations governing Press coverage are contained in yet another annex with the instruction that Press aircraft must not fly lower than 500-ft when passing overhead, nor closer than 600-ft when flying past – and they are not allowed to dive on the Yacht. This last ruling might seem unnecessary but it is quite extraordinary the lengths to which some photographers will go to obtain pictures of The Queen and her family. The use of helicopters when *Britannia* is entering or leaving harbour is discouraged as the noise from their engines and rotors reduces the effectiveness of the band. The downdraft from rotor blades can also cause chaos with hats and skirts – Royal or otherwise.

All these and many more details were negotiated by Captain Voute, working literally as a one-man band. The Naval Attaché has no extra staff to call on so does everything himself.

Eventually everything was ready and the State Visit began. All went according to plan as it usually does with Royal

events, until the final evening. On the Friday, The Queen and the Duke of Edinburgh attended various functions in the city of Barcelona, together with the King and Queen of Spain. The plan was that a large reception would be held on board *Britannia* in the early evening, to be followed by a private dinner for Their Majesties, and a ceremonial departure.

The 200 non-Royal guests at the reception were invited to arrive half an hour before The King and Queen. They were all directed via specially devised routes, each accompanied by one of the Yacht's officers, so that there would be no traffic jam as they approached the ante-room where The Queen and Prince Philip were waiting to greet each one individually.

Peter Voute and Rear-Admiral Sir John Garnier (then Flag Officer Royal Yachts, now Private Secretary to Princess Alexandra) were waiting on the Royal gangway, meeting the VIP guests and introducing them to their host officers. Guards had been posted all along the approaching jetty. They were equipped with walkie-talkie radios to warn the Yacht of King Juan Carlos'

Starting to encounter rough seas. Britannia's stabilisers enable her to cope with practically any conditions, but there have been times when even The Queen has been forced to remain in her cabin.

impending arrival so that those on board could tell Prince Philip in plenty of time for him to get to the gangway to welcome Their Majesties.

Peter Voute takes up the story: 'Everything seemed to be going smoothly; the most important guests were being fed faster into the system so that they could meet The Queen more or less as they arrived, when all of a sudden – at around half past seven – a voice came through on one of the radios saying "The King is coming, The King is coming". We replied, "Don't be so bloody stupid, he's not due until eight o'clock, there's another half hour to go". But sure enough, with blue flashing lights, police escort, outriders and everything else, The King suddenly arrived with The Queen, half an hour early.

'It was absolute chaos. I managed to get a message through to the Duke of Edinburgh who was with The Queen in the receiving room and it was the only time I've ever seen His Royal Highness actually run, which is what he had to do to get to the gangway in time to greet The King and Queen. But he did it, and by the time Their Majesties had got out

of their car the Duke was there to welcome them aboard and it was just as if he had been waiting all along. A minor hiccup and quite funny really. Everything went fine after that.

'The reception continued, then there was a dinner party followed by Beat Retreat on the quayside which was watched by thousands of Barcelonian people who were allowed on to the jetty.

'After the band had re-embarked and King Juan Carlos and Queen Sofia had left, the Yacht prepared to leave the harbour, totally floodlit and the band playing once more. The Queen and the Duke of Edinburgh stand in a specially designated spot on deck, waving goodbye and gradually the lights dim so that all that is left is a floodlight on the Royal couple and they are the last thing the people on shore see – it's pure theatre and very dramatic'.

Britannia was making the short voyage to Palma de Majorca overnight. Peter Voute and his wife raced to the airport to catch a late flight to Palma where they were on the jetty next morning when the Yacht arrived. The harbour at Palma is one of the most spectacular in the world. Hundreds of

The ship's company wear soft-soled plimsoles at all times and orders are given by hand signal to preserve the tranquillity required in a Royal residence. Shouting is forbidden. She is equipped with the latest satellite communications systems and on the Royal Bridge a special mahogany windbreak has been built to prevent any sea breezes from blowing up the Royal skirts.

yachts, fishing boats, cargo vessels and luxury liners tie up alongside one of the most beautiful promenades, dominated at one end by the magnificent cathedral.

Britannia's Commander, Admiral Garnier, brought her in, tied her up and the crew were preparing for the gangways to go down as The Queen and Prince Philip were getting ready to go ashore to join King Juan Carlos and Queen Sofia for a short holiday. The State Visit was over; now was a time for relaxation.

Peter Voute was just starting to cross into the Yacht via the working gangway which is always the first to be lowered – the Royal gangway comes later – when the barriers guarding the entrance to the jetty parted and up drove an open-topped car with the King and Queen of Spain inside. It was totally unexpected and completely unannounced. King Juan Carlos was so excited at the prospect of The Queen coming to his beloved Majorca, where he has a Summer Palace at Marevent, that he could not wait for the protocol to be observed. He just turned up having flown over from Barcelona the previous night.

Luckily The Queen and Prince Philip were almost ready and in spite of having their pre-arranged programme turned upside down they fell in with The King's plans with good humour. The Queen joined King Juan Carlos in the front of his car and they went for a drive around Palma. When the 'post mortem' was held into the Spanish visit, back in London, it was agreed that it was one of the most successful and – for The Queen – enjoyable ever undertaken.

Before Her Majesty left Spain she gave King Juan Carlos the Order of the Garter – her own personal Order of Chivalry – and a water-colour by the artist Norman Wilkinson showing yachts sailing at Cowes. This was specially chosen by The Queen, knowing His Majesty's love of sailing. She also gave Queen Sofia an original manuscript of an Oratorio by Mozart. Their son, the Prince of the Asturias, was made a Knight Grand Cross of the Royal Victorian Order (GCVO).

There was one incident which could have been uncomfortable. It concerned the morning service held on board *Britannia* on the Sunday. Two ships were escorting the Royal Yacht, one from the Royal Navy and the second from the Spanish Navy, and in Palma they were both berthed behind *Britannia*. The Queen always invites the crews of her escort ships to join her at Sunday worship. On this occasion she extended the invitation to the Spaniards also. Being Roman Catholic the captain was apparently in a dilemma as he did not wish to attend a Protestant service, neither did he want to send any of his crew. Finally he decided it would be better all round if he declined the invitation. The crew of *HMS Apollo*, the British escort ship were the only ones to turn up.

The Queen did not mention the subject again and the matter was considered to be closed. In fact it emerged later that the real reason why the captain of the Spanish escort had refused the invitation was that most of his crew were national service conscripts and he feared their turnout would not be nearly as smart as that of *Britannia*'s. He had already had a taste of what might happen because he had selected half a dozen of his sailors to be presented to The Queen at the end of the Barcelona part of the visit and one of the younger men was so overcome by the prospect of meeting Her Majesty that he passed out at her feet. So it was national pride not religious intolerance that prevented a seemingly harmless ecumenical get-together, but the incident did not mar the overall success of the visit in any way.

Shortly before *Britannia* departed on the Monday morning all the people who had worked on the visit – embassy staff, port officials and anyone else who had helped – were invited to meet The Queen in the Drawing Room. There she thanked them personally and handed them gifts appropriate to their rank. The British Ambassador, Nicholas Gordon Lennox (now Lord Gordon Lennox) was knighted.

Peter Voute was delighted to receive two presents: a pair of gold cuff links engraved with the Royal cypher, in a red leather box, and a signed photograph in a blue leather frame of The Queen and the Duke of Edinburgh. Captain Voute had been warned in advance that he was going to be given something but was not told what it would be. The quality of the gifts showed his standing and how much The Queen recognised his efforts on her behalf.

Her Majesty likes to show her appreciation to those who work behind the scenes. A selection of presents is taken along on every State Visit. In 1991 their cost amounted to £34,000. The presents rarely change: cuff links and wallets for the men, brooches and powder boxes for the ladies. There are framed photographs of herself for the chosen few,

Her Majesty arriving at her floating palace, the one place in the world where she can truly relax.
(Photographers International)

who can tell immediately how highly they are regarded (or to be more accurate, what their rank and social standing are) by the quality of the frames. Silver is for Heads of State and ambassadors, blue leather for recipients of 'senior management' status, and brown leather for those who just about make it into the 'personal photograph' league.

When the gifts are being packed for transit aboard *Britannia* they are listed by the Master of the Household in the following order:

Picture Frame (A) Silver – stamped with cypher.

Picture Frame (B) Blue leather – stamped with cypher.

Picture Frame (C) Blue leather – unstamped.

Picture Frame (D) Brown leather – unstamped.

Powder Box (A) Square silver box with raised Royal cypher in centre in a stamped red leather box.

Powder Box (B) Small, round, silver, with cypher engraved in centre. Unstamped box.

Cuff Links (A) Gold, with cypher on both links. Red stamped box.

Cuff Links (B) Gold, oval, with cypher. Red stamped box.

Cuff Links (C) Gold, with cut corners. Cypher in blue enamel, flush. Royal blue box, stamped.

Wallet (A) Pigskin, embossed with cypher. Unstamped box.

Wallet (B) Brown, pin seal, fitted with gold corners. Cypher in top right hand corner. Unstamped box.

The Royal Household have their own names for the presents, particularly the photographs which they refer to as: Large Blue Pair. This means Picture Frame (B), the pair are two pictures of The Queen and the Duke of Edinburgh on facing pages. A Small Blue Joint is Picture Frame (C), and is a single photograph of the Royal couple. A Large Brown Joint is the same photograph in a slightly larger frame but in the infinitely lower category of brown leather.

For the crew of *Britannia* this was just another voyage, another State Visit. The amount of planning and organisation that had gone into the smooth running of the operation was routine as far as they were concerned. They have been doing it for so long now that there is very little that can throw them out of their stride.

However, for people in the host country, including the British Embassy staff, this was a one-off occasion that had taken an extraordinary amount of work. Many of them had toiled long hours to ensure that The Queen and Prince Philip's visit would be a success, some of them working at tasks which would normally have been right out of their usual areas of competence. Typists became flower arrangers, second secretaries became messengers, and even Naval Attachés became dockyard labourers for a day.

In the end it was all worth it, especially when The Queen offered a few personal words of thanks and gave a small memento of her visit. The intrinsic value of the gift did not matter; what counted was the fact that by giving it, Her Majesty had shown the thoughtfulness of a sovereign who, though she appears to accept perfection as the norm, fully appreciates the lengths to which people will go to make her life and work as comfortable as possible.

THE LOVE BOAT?

PRINCESS MARGARET AND her husband Antony Armstrong-Jones were the first Royal couple to use *Britannia* for a honeymoon. On 6 May 1960 they stepped into the Royal Barge at Tower Pier for the start of a 6,000 mile voyage to the Caribbean.

Britannia was waiting in the Pool of London and as they set sail down river,

under Tower Bridge, vast crowds of well-wishers waved to them from the shore. On board, the Band of the Royal Marines was playing one of the hit tunes of the day, *Oh What a Beautiful Morning*.

The Queen had offered the use of the Royal Yacht so that the newlyweds could enjoy some privacy at the start of their married life together, but even

Four Royal honeymoons have been spent on Britannia, *which gave rise to some of the crew naming her the 'Love Boat'. As all four marriages have now broken up, the title is no longer considered appropriate.*

then this most controversial of all items of Royal expenditure attracted criticism from a Member of Parliament. The Labour MP Emrys Hughes asked questions in the House of Commons about the cost of the honeymoon and the use of the Royal Yacht. He was told that there were 20 officers and 337 Yachtsmen on board (more than a third more than the present complement) and that they were paid a total of £4,000 a week in wages whether they sailed or not, so the honeymoon was not involving *Britannia* in any extra expense.

The official answer neglected to add that there was the cost of bringing *Britannia* from Portsmouth to London, embarking the Royal couple and their entourage, and then taking them on a round trip to the Caribbean. Anyway, the Civil Lord of the Admiralty dismissed the question by saying that Princess Margaret deserved the voyage in view of the extraordinary amount of work she had undertaken on behalf of the country.

As this was the first Royal honeymoon cruise, the Admiral commanding the Yacht had issued special instructions regarding the privacy of Princess Margaret and her husband. They were to be left completely alone at all times. All work near their apartments was to be carried out in silence and none to be started before nine o'clock in the morning.

In 1960 there was still enormous formality at Court and this was carried through onto *Britannia*. Princess Margaret did not, and still does not, encourage familiarity from any of the crew, neither did she wish to join in with any informal entertainments held on board. Her idea of a honeymoon cruise was to be left in complete privacy, and for the standards she had become used to ashore to be maintained at all times.

Whereas, 20 years later, the Princess of Wales was to be found wondering about the Yacht bare-foot or joining the deck hands in their mess for a drink and a sing-song, Princess Margaret confined herself to the Royal Apartments, and the only glimpse any member of the crew had of her in a swimsuit was when she was served with a cool drink on the Verandah Deck as she lay sun-bathing.

All meals were taken in the State Dining Room. Lunch was served with the same amount of ceremony that was to be found in Buckingham Palace. Each night the Princess and her husband dined in formal surroundings, he wearing dinner jacket and she in full length evening gown, complete with jewels and tiara. They were joined at dinner by a Lady-in-Waiting and Private Secretary, also in evening dress, with the Flag Officer Royal Yachts and one or two senior officers occasionally being invited to join them.

For the Princess it was the best of both worlds: she was able to enjoy the privacy she craved without giving up any of the comforts she had always been used to.

The crew went to great lengths to provide a romantic atmosphere, and *Britannia* was successful in avoiding most of the pursuing pack of Press photographers, all of whom wanted that elusive, exclusive picture of Princess Margaret in a swimsuit. They visited

'My wife said there was no way she was not going to come on board the Royal Yacht and see where The Queen lives.' Even the most successful business people find it hard to turn down an opportunity to see for themselves what life is like on board the most exclusive yacht in the world.

islands like Tobago, Antigua and Mustique, where American, French and Italian papparazzi did their best to catch the couple unawares. The British Press had not at that time caught up with their foreign colleagues in matters of intrusive reporting. They were more discreet in their coverage of the honeymoon.

Britannia's crew had been sworn to secrecy about the movements and any other details they might have learned of the Royal couple during their time on board. But, inevitably, word leaked out that they had adjoining state rooms and that a double bed had been installed in Princess Margaret's cabin (this was proved to be false, as is the story that Royal honeymooners have to bring their own double bed. *Britannia* has always had a double bed available in one of the cabins on the Shelter Deck).

It was further revealed that after dinner they liked to sit on the Verandah Deck listening to Frank Sinatra and Nat King Cole records. This was no great secret as Princess Margaret had never disguised her love for this kind of middle of the road music. They enjoyed reading, but never paperbacks, and only hardbacks which had never been opened before. A selection of the latest best sellers had been brought along including *The Longest Day* and Joy Adamson's *Born Free*.

Reporters also learned that Sylvia Davies, a stylist from Rene's hairdressing salon in London, was on board throughout the voyage. Again this was nothing out of the ordinary; all Royal ladies take their hairdresser with them on overseas trips. Intimate details of Princess Margaret's underwear were leaked – or invented – apparently, it consisted of hand-woven Crêpe de Chine, while her nightdresses were sheer silk. Antony Armstrong-Jones

wore pyjamas and a silk dressing gown, and his favourite nickname for his wife was 'Ducky'. All fairly harmless information but an indication of the kind of detail that newspapers would increasingly demand in years to come.

As with all Royal occasions the honeymoon cruise went like clockwork. The weather was kind, nobody suffered any seasickness, there were no unpleasant incidents and if, when they arrived back in Portsmouth at the end of their three-week cruise, Mr Armstrong-Jones was a little surprised at the size of the turnout to greet them, and the formality of the welcoming ceremonies, he successfully concealed any reservations he may have had.

Before leaving *Britannia* the Princess and her husband thanked the Admiral and asked him to convey their appreciation to the officers and Yachtsmen for the manner in which they had all gone out of their way to make this honeymoon such a memorable occasion.

ROMANCE WAS LAST THING IN MIND

It was to be 13 years before *Britannia* was again asked, or instructed, to act as a floating honeymoon hotel. In November 1973 The Queen's only daughter Princess Anne (now The Princess Royal) married Captain Mark Phillips of 1st The Queen's Dragoon Guards. Once again Her Majesty had offered the use of the Royal Yacht which was en route to New Zealand in preparation for a State Visit by The Queen and the Duke of Edinburgh early the following year. No great extra expense was incurred as *Britannia* was already in the West Indies. All it meant was that the Princess and Captain Phillips had to fly from London to Barbados where they joined the Yacht.

Overnight was busy. The Royal Apartments were cleared in preparation for the accommodation of an unknown number of evacuees, and communications had to be established with the British Embassy in Aden.

A West Indies cruise aboard the world's finest private yacht may seem the perfect way for any young couple to start their married life together, even if it did mean sharing the ship with 21 officers and 256 Yachtsmen. But even a captain who is in reality a Rear-Admiral cannot legislate against the weather, and for the first part of the honeymoon violent storms rocked the West Indies. There were 20-foot waves against which *Britannia's* stabilisers were useless; vicious thunder and lightning storms with continuous rain made it impossible to venture out on deck, and for most of that first week Anne and Mark spent all their time in bed – apart. Both suffered severe seasickness. Romance was the last thing on either of their minds.

However, the storms eventually subsided, the sun came out and the honeymoon progressed as planned, with *Britannia* island-hopping once more throughout the West Indies, playing games of hide-and-seek with the hordes of Press reporters and photographers who were following the yacht in a fleet of specially chartered craft. It was a much more serious and well organised attempt to penetrate the Royal defences. But this time there were no important leaks and few details emerged of the way in which the couple spent their days and nights on board.

Princess Anne had made her first voyage on *Britannia* when she was barely two years old and she had been on board at least once every year since. She had even held her 21st birthday party on *Britannia* in 1971, so she was thoroughly familiar with the Yacht and knew many of the Permanent Yachtsmen personally. She was, and remains, very much aware of her position within the Royal Family, but in sharp contrast to Princess Margaret, Princess Anne enjoyed the company of the ship's officers and even shared a joke with the crew when the occasion warranted. She has always liked the earthy humour of sailors. When she spoke at the Yacht's annual dinner in Portsmouth in 1990, she reminded them of some of the jokes they had played on her, both on her honeymoon and on other voyages.

As with all voyages when Royalty is embarked, the couple were mainly left to themselves except when the Admiral joined them once every day with his charts to show them where they were, how far they had travelled in the night, and to make suggestions about suitable islands and beaches they might like to visit for picnics or swimming.

During the latter part of the honeymoon cruise – which also included a number of official engagements in Antigua, Jamaica, Montserrat and Colombia – the Stewards of the Royal Apartments went out of their way to try to make up for the disappointment of the first week. Special menus were arranged and candlelit dinners on the Verandah Deck, where soft lights had been installed, were organised just for the two of them. Princess Anne is not sentimental normally, and the champagne was wasted on her as she does not drink, but even she was touched by the efforts of the crew to create a romantic atmosphere, and by all accounts, it worked.

Mark Phillips said afterwards that every man dreams of being able to take his bride on such a honeymoon: in his case he had to thank his mother-in-law for making his dream come true.

When the Prince and Princess of Wales joined *Britannia* for their 16-day honeymoon cruise in 1981 it was truly a fairy-tale beginning to their marriage. They had spent their first night together at Broadlands, the Hampshire home of Lord Louis Mountbatten, and then flew in an Andover of The Queen's Flight to Gibraltar where the Royal Yacht was waiting for them.

Unlike most honeymoon couples, the Waleses had not had to arrange their own transport or do their own packing. They simply had to turn up. Prince Charles's valet and the Princess's dresser travelled with them, and had supervised the packing of everything that would be needed during the voyage, weeks before. The Prince and Princess occupied the cabins on the Shelter Deck with its colour scheme of white with red upholstery and silver grey carpets. The Queen had given the Princess of Wales permis-

sion to use her own bedroom as a dressing room.

As they set sail through the Mediterranean the tone of the voyage was decided by Prince Charles himself. Wherever he is in the world, he is an early riser and is always called by 7.30 a.m. at the latest, usually much earlier outside London. Now, for the first time ever, his valet had been told not to wake him in the morning but to wait until he was summoned by the bell alongside the couple's bed. When the bell rang it was usually after eight and then the steward would wheel the breakfast trolley into the bedroom and leave them to serve themselves. This was going to be the pattern for the cruise, no rigid, inflexible routine but a completely informal holiday which was enjoyed not only by the Royal couple themselves but also by their servants and *Britannia*'s crew.

The Princess of Wales chose all their meals in consultation with the Royal chef, and as they were sailing in temper-

The Princess of Wales' luggage being carried on board just before the start of the honeymoon cruise. (Jayne Fincher)

atures of around 90 degrees Fahrenheit, most of it was cold food, with ice cream served as dessert after nearly every meal. They drank the occasional glass of champagne, a little light German white wine, no red wine at all as Prince Charles will not drink it even with beef, and lots of his favourite English sparkling mineral water. It was the closest the Prince of Wales had ever come to informal living – and he loved every moment of it!

Apart from one evening in Port Said, when President Sadat of Egypt and his wife came on board for a private dinner, the formal State Apartments were rarely used, the Prince and Princess preferring to use the Sun Lounge on the Shelter Deck, or sunbathing on the sheltered Verandah Deck.

The Princess spent most of the days in her bikini. If she decided she wanted to go 'walk-about' through the rest of the yacht she would slip a simple summer skirt over her swimsuit. She enjoyed exploring *Britannia*'s lower

A member of Prince Charles' personal staff carries his master's vegetables onto Britannia. *The Prince of Wales has his own private stock, all grown at Highgrove under organic conditions.* (Jayne Fincher)

A poignant reminder of happier times. (Jayne Fincher)

decks. The crew soon became used to the sight of her peering into cupboards and cabins, messdecks and galleys. At 20, she was the same age as many of the Yachtsmen and an easy camaraderie grew up between the newest member of the Royal Family and the crew. Most of the Yachtsmen suffered some form of 'Dianamania'. They vied with each other in telling stories of how she had made some personal remark or shared a joke. One of the sailors was convinced that he had been singled out by the Princess for special attention, claiming she always smiled at him, even across a crowded messroom. The fact that he happened to be six feet five inches tall and that this may have had something to do with it, somehow escaped him.

Some of the more senior Petty Officers were more protective of their

visitor. On one occasion, when the Princess had joined in a sing-song in one of the junior messes, even giving them a solo performance of *Greensleeves* on the piano, then leading them in *What Shall We Do With The Drunken Sailor*, they discreetly but firmly led her back to her own part of the Yacht.

Years of Royal training had instilled in Prince Charles reservations about going where he wasn't expected, and he remained in the Royal Apartments throughout the honeymoon voyage. It simply would not have occurred to him to do otherwise. The only occasion when he ventured into the 'HMS Britannia' side of the Yacht was when he and the Princess were formally invited to tour the ship and visit the Ward Room.

It wasn't a question of snobbery; it was just that he would have been

Britannia in Port Said, Egypt, during the honeymoon of the Prince and Princess of Wales. They interrupted their holiday for an official visit with President Anwar Sadat who made them very welcome. (Jayne Fincher)

uncomfortable if he was discovered poking around 'below stairs', just as he would in any of the Royal residences ashore. It's the same today with The Queen and Princess Margaret. They were brought up to respect the privacy of their servants and they would no more invade the kitchens or sitting rooms of their staff uninvited than they would expect staff to visit their own private apartments.

As *Britannia* cruised along the North African coast en route for the Greek Isles, they would stop occasionally for the Prince and Princess to go ashore for a picnic and to swim. Even on such an informal holiday as this though there were formalities that had to be observed. Before the Royal couple could be allowed ashore one of *Britannia*'s small boats would carry out a 'recce' to make sure the site was suitable and that there were no sightseers around. A ship's officer, several boatmen, one of the Royal police officers and the Prince's valet would go ashore first of all to see that the designated spot was deserted. They would then make elaborate preparations

for the picnic lunch and only then would the Prince and Princess follow on. Throughout the brief stay ashore, the two police officers on duty would maintain a watching brief over their Royal charges from a discreet distance; far enough away to allow some degree of privacy, but near enough should any emergency arise.

When *Britannia* anchored in secluded bays the Princess of Wales would swim alone at the stern of the Yacht while the staff and crew used the other end. Prince Charles rarely ventured into the sea, although he is a strong swimmer and enthusiastic wind-surfer, preferring to stay on deck sunbathing. The late Stephen Barry, the Prince's valet at the time, said that his boss was very proud of his tan and the fact that he did not need suntan lotion to protect his skin. On one occasion, the valet, who was also getting nicely brown, said the Prince told him, 'You're getting browner than me'. To which the immediate and diplomatic reply was, 'Oh, no Sir, you are much more tanned than any of us'.

Both the Prince and Princess took

The Princess of Wales in Sardinia with the then FORY Rear-Admiral (now Sir) Paul Greening who went on to become Master of the Household. (Jayne Fincher)

Four years after they were married the Prince and Princess of Wales were again on Britannia *sailing to Sardinia.* (Jayne Fincher)

lots of photographs – with varying degrees of success. The only other camera allowed on board was that of 'Snaps', the ship's official photographer. All private cameras had been banned for the duration of the cruise. It was considered politic not to place too much temptation before the crew, especially as the tabloid Press would have offered thousands (they still will) for any revealing pictures of the Princess.

As always, *Britannia* was shadowed by an escort, a Royal Navy frigate, which kept watch from a respectable distance, only catching up when it was necessary to deliver mail or official documents which needed Prince Charles's attention. Even on honeymoon the business of monarchy never stops. The Prince of Wales spent a part of most days working on his papers.

Also, his Assistant Private Secretary, Francis Cornish, would fly out to join the Yacht at various points in the voyage. His main task was to make sure there were no problems with customs or immigration in the countries they visited. He also acted as Prince Charles's representative when it became necessary to pay courtesy calls.

Cornish really had the best of both worlds even if it did involve a lot of flying between England and the ports where he met the Royal Yacht. He would be picked up by one of the Yacht's boats, taken out to *Britannia*, where he would spend a couple of hours going over the business of the day with the Prince, then enjoy a meal with the officers in the Ward Room, have a swim or join the others for a barbecue and spend perhaps just one night in one of the very comfortable cabins the Household uses just below the Royal deck.

When *Britannia* reached the Greek Isles, the officers in the Ward Room organised a beach barbecue at which they prepared and cooked all the food. Everyone was invited, including Prince Charles's personal chef, who was given a break from choosing and cooking something different for his Royal employers every day. He just sat back and let the others get on with it. The Prince and Princess were of course the guests of honour. A large bonfire was lit on the beach so they could all sit around it and sing camp-fire songs, and they joined in with gusto. Just to make sure they all knew the words the officers had had song sheets printed, and to make doubly sure everyone was in tune, an accordionist from the Yacht's band was brought ashore to lead the singers. Such is the efficiency and attention to detail that characterises even the most informal entertainment when Royalty are involved.

One of the truly amazing things about this honeymoon cruise was that in 16 days sailing in one of the most popular holiday areas in the world, not once were they bothered by other ships or intrusive helicopters, and on their expeditions ashore they did not see a single person in any of the islands they visited.

For the Prince and Princess it was the most relaxing time of their lives. Never again would they share such idyllic moments together, secure in the knowledge that they could do and say what they liked without any possibility of being seen or overheard by the media. They didn't know it at the time, but this was to be among the most precious couple of weeks of the next 10 years.

The honeymoon ended at Hurghada in Egypt. The crew of *Britannia* lined the decks and cheered as the Royal couple left the Yacht to fly back to Britain in an RAF VC10. Everyone, crew and guests, had enjoyed a wonderful occasion; now it was back to work. The Yacht sailed on to Melbourne, Australia, where it was to meet The Queen who was opening the 1981 Commonwealth Conference. The Prince and Princess of Wales were returning to Scotland to join other members of the Royal Family at Balmoral.

In 1986 there was a fourth Royal honeymoon on board *Britannia* when the Duke and Duchess of York took over the Royal suite for five days. The Royal Yacht had sailed from its home base at Portsmouth to position in Praia de Vitoria in the Azores ready to welcome the couple after their wedding in Westminster Abbey.

An aircraft of The Queen's Flight – the first time one of the new BAe 146s had been used – flew them from London's Heathrow Airport to the joint Portuguese/American airbase at Lajes where they arrived exactly on schedule at 8 p.m.

Hundreds of cheering people lined the short route from the airbase to the port where *Britannia*, dressed overall, lay at anchor, 200 yards offshore.

With the minimum of formalities – just a charming send-off from the Mayor and a couple of government representatives – the newlyweds embarked in the Royal Barge for the short trip to the

> *The Queen does not make a regular habit of asking her officers to join her for meals; her Ladies-in-Waiting and Private Secretaries usually dine with the family and the Commodore is in attendance.*

Yacht and the honeymoon was under way.

The schedule was undecided until the last moment. The Admiral had certain suggestions to make but the final decisions were left to the couple themselves. The Duke of York had let it be known that he had some ideas himself as he had been in the area during his service in the Falklands campaign.

Within 90 minutes of the couple's arrival in the Azores, *Britannia* had sailed – for destinations unknown. Wherever they were going it seemed an inspired choice for newlyweds who wanted to get away from it all. There are nine islands in this Portuguese archipelago, 2,000 miles from Britain, and all of them inaccessible without local knowledge.

The Yacht had received permission to land at three islands in the group: Faial,

Sao Jorge and Pico. But the pursuing Press party, numbering over 100, could only guess if *Britannia* was actually going to anchor at any of them or if it was an elaborate decoy.

The media had decided to really go to town on this occasion but they were out of luck. There were no private helicopters or aircraft available for hire, just a few motor cruisers and even these were fetching up to £3,000 a week.

In addition there was the problem of trying to elude the attentions of the Portuguese navy who had provided three armed escort ships to deter intruders. One local fisherman who the Press were trying to tempt into taking them after *Britannia*, declined saying, 'I have been warned that the navy will shoot at anything that comes within 200 yards of the Royal Yacht'.

The younger Royals on board. When Prince William and Prince Harry waited for their parents to arrive in Toronto, Admiral Woodard kept a friendly eye on them. (Jayne Fincher)

It was probably the most successful of all Royal honeymoons held on board in terms of the privacy they were able to enjoy; and the least successful from the media's point of view.

Some of the islands were so isolated that the only way the Duke and Duchess could get ashore to picnic on the deserted beaches was to use one of the Yacht's inflatable rubber dinghies. Prince Andrew thoroughly enjoyed displaying his seamanship on these occasions, though what the Duchess thought of her husband's technique has never been revealed. They both went skin-diving in the calm, crystal clear waters around the islands and tried their hands at deep-sea fishing for marlin, with varying degrees of success.

Britannia's crew knew what was expected of them and they were delight-ed to give the Royal couple all the space they wanted. And with only two principal guests – plus a tiny entourage of dresser, valet, private secretary and police officers, who kept out of the way most of the time, unless invited to join in – it was the perfect way to spend a honeymoon. The brilliant sunshine and dramatic backdrop of the volcanic islands, combined with the superb food and wines served on board the finest private yacht in the world, all helped to create a romantic atmosphere.

There were one or two disappointed local dignitaries who had hoped to be able to welcome the newlyweds ashore on their own islands. But all the invitations, which were relayed to the Yacht by the Portuguese navy, were politely declined. The Duke of York was determined that the newest member of the

Three generations of Royalty on board as the Duke and Duchess of York show their first daughter Princess Beatrice to her grandmother, The Queen. (Jayne Fincher)

Royal Family was not going to have her first impression of *Britannia*, and the sort of lifestyle she could expect from then on, spoiled by having to go through the rigmarole of official handshaking, receptions and formal functions during this most private of occasions.

The nearest they came to an official duty was towards the end of the five-day cruise when they anchored at Sao Miguel, their final port of call. Here they received on board the President of the Azores regional government, Dr Joso Amaral, and several of his colleagues who were anxious to present greetings from the people of the Azores and to thank the Duke and Duchess for choosing their islands for the honeymoon cruise.

The couple stayed on board for the return journey to England arriving in Portsmouth Harbour on 3 August 1986. The crowds who lined the shore-line at Cowes on the Isle of Wight were not even sure if they were on board as there had been no confirmation. And the Press were nearly fooled when the Duke's Equerry, Wing Commander Adam Wise, accompanied by a young woman looking remarkably like the Duchess of York, appeared on the bridge as the Yacht entered Portsmouth.

A flotilla of media boats, pleasure craft, sailing dinghies and yachts circled *Britannia* as the real Duke and Duchess suddenly walked out on to the Verandah Deck, holding hands, dressed in casual sports clothes. Smiling broadly, they waved to the onlookers, acknowledged

Without doubt one of the happiest pictures ever taken on the Royal Yacht. The Princess of Wales forgets all Royal protocol and rushes to hug her sons as she arrives in Toronto. (Jayne Fincher)

the salutes of the other boats in the welcoming party for a few minutes, and when everyone had got their pictures they went back inside. It was a good humoured end to a wonderful cruise and *Britannia* was immediately back on duty as host ship for Prince Philip at Cowes Week.

But it was to be only a few days before the Duke and Duchess of York were to be reunited with the Yacht. The Queen invited them to join her for the Western Isles cruise and they were clever enough to slip aboard without being seen by the horde of reporters and cameramen waiting at Southampton.

Britannia is of course the perfect choice for a honeymoon. Everyone on board knows that The Queen and her family value their privacy greatly and so they perform their duties as silently and quickly as possible. They are there if needed, 24 hours a day. When they are not required they keep well out of the way. The Royal Apartments are run like the very best five star hotels: maximum efficiency, minimum fuss. But unlike any hotel no matter how efficient, this one goes where the clients want it to go, and when they want it to go – and you cannot beat that!

A PROUD HISTORY

PRINCE PHILIP HAS written that *Britannia* is the first Royal Yacht to be built with a complete ocean-going capacity and fitted out specifically as an 'official' Royal residence with facilities for the reception and entertainment of guests at home and abroad. Prior to this, commercial passenger liners were chartered or one of the Royal Navy's warships commandeered whenever a Royal tour overseas was being undertaken.

Since the 17th century British sovereigns have had Official, if not Royal, Yachts and, indeed, some kings made a habit of collecting yachts, amassing a dozen or more in their lifetime.

Altogether there have been seven ships in the Royal Navy bearing the name *Britannia*. The first was a warship of 1,703 tons, armed with 100 guns and manned by a crew of 780 men. She was built at Chatham in 1682 by Phineas Pett, and served as a battleship of the English Fleet for more than half a century before ending her days as a hospital ship at Queenborough. She was broken up at Chatham in 1749. How appropriate then that the new *Britannia* was also originally intended to be used as a hospital ship in time of war. In fact she never did fulfil that role and eventually, in 1992, it was officially decided that it would be impracticable for her to do so

and the idea was dropped once and for all.

The second *Britannia* was an armed storeship of 535 tons with 20 guns, but she had a short sea life. Having been purchased in 1781, she was wrecked on the Kentish Knock less than a year later. Paradoxically the third ship to bear the name was launched in 1762 at Portsmouth as a 1st Rate battleship of 2,091 tons, carrying 100 guns and 850 men. She saw action in Gibraltar in 1781, again in 1793 against the French at Toulon, and Genoa in 1795. She took part in the Battle of Cape St. Vincent on 14 February 1797 and her most celebrated battle of all was Trafalgar, on 21 October 1805, as the Flagship of Rear-Admiral The Earl of Northesk, when 10 of her crew were killed and 42 wounded.

The fourth *Britannia* was built at Plymouth and launched in October

For the Prince and Princess it was the most relaxing time of their lives. Never again would they share such idyllic moments together, secure in the knowledge that they could do and say what they liked without any possibility of being seen or overheard by the media.

1820. Another 1st Rate warship, of 2,616 tons, she carried 120 guns and was involved in the Crimea in 1854 when she took part in the bombardment of Sebastopol as the Flagship of Vice-Admiral Dundas. In 1858 she became a Cadets Training Ship and paid off at Devonport in 1869 when she was broken up.

There were two other ships which were to carry the name *Britannia* before the present Royal Yacht. The first was the *Prince of Wales* which was renamed *Britannia* in 1869 when she replaced the previously mentioned vessel as Cadets Training Ship, and then in 1904, the battleship *Britannia* was launched. She was a massive 16,350 tons and armed with 12-in and 9.2-in guns. During the First World War she saw active service in the North Atlantic with the 3rd Battle Squadron and 9th Cruiser Squadron before coming to a tragic end just two days before the end of hostilities. She was sunk by a German submarine off Cape Trafalgar on 9 November 1918.

So, nearly 35 years later, when The Queen gave this proud name to her new Royal Yacht, she was not only continuing a long and distinguished custom, but also ensuring that a name which had first been introduced into the Royal Navy in the 17th century would remain in the forefront of Britain's maritime tradition for the rest of the 20th century.

In other ways the naming of the Royal Yacht was a break with tradition as the last three Royal Yachts had all borne the name *Victoria & Albert*. They, of course, had been built in the reign of Queen Victoria and had been used not only by her but by her successors, Edward VII, George V and George VI, all of whom could remember their illustrious ancestor and were equally anxious not to do anything to upset

those precious memories.

However, Elizabeth II, who was born in 1926 and came to the throne in 1952, was determined that the Yacht – considered originally by her father, King George VI, just before the outbreak of the Second World War – would herald the start of the new Elizabethan era in the modern post-war period not by immortalising her own Christian name, or that of her husband, but by recalling a name which had symbolised the might of Britain's naval power for 300 years. 'Britannia Rules the Waves' had been no idle boast in the past, and Her Majesty saw no reason why, in peacetime, the ship which was to steam more than a million miles in her lifetime, should not carry this proud name to the four corners of the earth.

Britannia is the sixty-sixth Royal Yacht in a line that reaches back to 1660 when King Charles II, the newly restored monarch, took possession of his first yacht. He named her the *Mary*, after his sister who had become the first Princess Royal in 1642. The *Mary* was a gift from the people of Amsterdam where the King had spent his years in exile and she arrived in the Thames just two months after His Majesty returned

The Royal Coat of Arms which was salvaged from the second of Queen Victoria's Royal steam yachts, the Victoria & Albert II, *which served from 1855–1901.* (Courtesy H.M. Yacht)

to England to claim his Throne. This first Royal Yacht, some 50-ft long, had a crew of 30 and was part of a large fleet of yachts owned by the King in his lifetime. None of them was ocean-going in the sense that we use the phrase today and most were used principally for sport. The King loved to race, particularly against his brother, the Duke of York, for large sums.

The *Mary* was wrecked on the Skerries in 1675, and a second yacht the *Anne*, built in 1661, was sold in 1686, while the *Katherine*, another Royal Yacht manned by 30 men, was captured in 1673 by the Dutch – by that time at war with England – who also sank the *Henrietta* in the same year. The largest of King Charles II's 27 yachts was the *Saudadoes* built in 1673. This had a crew of 75 and was eventually captured by the French in 1696, by which time it was being used by the Navy as a warship, on the instructions of William III who had acceded to the throne in 1689.

In fact, no fewer than 25 of Charles II's yachts were eventually given to the Royal Navy and subsequently used in general service. Two of them, the *Merlin* and *Monmouth*, carried out one of the most important hydrographic tasks in British maritime history. They were used to complete the first survey of coastal waters around the British Isles. The survey, published in 1693, was used for the next 100 years and became the standard work on the subject.

Charles II was undoubtedly the first champion of Royal yachting. He was himself an excellent sailor, fully prepared to handle the sails or the helm in all winds and weathers. But he also enjoyed a sumptuous lifestyle which he saw no reason to abandon simply because he was on board ship. His yacht *Fubbs*, built in 1682, and subsequently rebuilt by William III in 1701, and again by George I in 1724, was the first Royal Yacht to contain anything like State Apartments. The ship had been named after the King's favourite mistress, the Duchess of Portsmouth, Fubbs being his pet name for her, and was the first to really justify the description of a 'Palace Afloat'. The master suite contained the most elegant four-poster bed with silk hangings and a head-board of intricately carved oak, and the decoration elsewhere throughout the yacht attracted praise from all who saw her.

It was to be more than 200 years before another British sovereign took anything like the same interest as Charles II in yachting, or even Royal Yachts. In the intervening period Royal Yachts were used mainly as a means of transportation across the English Channel and rarely for leisure cruises or racing.

MOST YACHTSMEN HAD OTHER JOBS

During the 18th century Royal Yachts looked more like small warships than the conventional perception of what a yacht should be. They were all armed and run on strictly naval lines with the correspondingly harsh discipline of the time. Men were flogged for the slightest transgression. The officers enjoyed a lifestyle which, though simple by modern standards, was as luxurious as money could make it (each officer providing his own furniture, food and wine, and frequently bringing his own personal servants on board). But the men below decks existed on a diet of hard-tack, any meat that the officers refused to eat, and whatever else they could scavenge for themselves.

Life in the navy has always been tough, and it was no easier simply because they were serving aboard a

The ornate and richly carved binnacle is well over 100 years old, having been in use in the old Victoria & Albert *and the* Royal George. *It now occupies a proud position overlooking the Verandah Deck.* (Courtesy H.M. Yacht)

Royal Yacht. The main advantage in those days was that unlike the other ships in the Royal Navy which undertook voyages of great length – up to a year away from home at times – the Royal Yacht usually only sailed in home waters or to one of the European ports, so the men had the opportunity of being with their families in England much more frequently than some of their fellow sailors in the warships. The majority of the Yachtsmen also had other jobs as riggers in Portsmouth Dockyard, to which they returned when they were not required for Royal duty.

The yacht which holds the record for the longest active career in Royal service is the *Royal Caroline* built in 1749. Renamed the *Royal Charlotte* in honour of Princess Charlotte of Mecklenburg-Strelitz, she brought the young princess back to England for her marriage to King George III. The *Royal Charlotte* sailed as a Royal Yacht until 1817 when the *Royal George* was built. In the official Admiralty records it is stated that she was 'taken to pieces' in 1820. Other Royal Yachts have been 'broken up' but there is a significant difference in the two terms. If a ship was 'taken to pieces' she was dismantled with great care and any parts that could be used again would be used in the construction of another ship. If a vessel was to be 'broken up', that is literally what happened.

The *Royal George* was a magnificent craft and was to be the last sailing Royal Yacht, apart from the smaller racing vessels used in later reigns. All the splendour of the Georgian period was captured in her decoration. There was lavish use of mahogany, lashings of gilt everywhere, and rich brocades used in the Royal Apartments. George III may have been an unpopular monarch but his subjects warmed to the idea of the new yacht and wherever she appeared huge crowds gathered to watch the King and his guests embarking. On her maiden voyage she was under the command of Sir Edward Berry, a vastly experienced seaman who had served under Nelson. Coincidentally, a gold button from Admiral Nelson's coat is displayed in the Ward Room on board the present Royal Yacht.

King George IV used the *Royal George* to travel to Scotland in 1822 where Sir Walter Scott was among those waiting to welcome him. But by the time Queen Victoria came to the throne in 1837, sail

A gold button taken from the uniform of Admiral Nelson occupies pride of place in Britannia's Ward Room. *(Courtesy H.M. Yacht)*

was already being overtaken by steam and Her Majesty used the *Royal George* only once. This was in 1842 and was also for a voyage to Scotland, sailing from Woolwich to Leith, the port of Edinburgh. In her journal for Monday, 29 August 1842, The Queen records:

At five o'clock in the morning we left Windsor . . . and arrived at Woolwich before seven . . . There was a large crowd to see us embark . . . I annex a list of our squadron [the escorting ships]

1. The ship *Pique*, 36 guns.
2. The sloop *Daphne*, 18 guns.
3. The steam vessel *Salamander* (with the carriages on board).
4. The steam vessel *Rhadamanthus* (Lord Liverpool and Lord Morton on board).
5. The steam vessel *Monkey*, a Tender, which has towed us till nine o'clock.
6. The steam vessel *Shearwater*, which is now towing us.
7. The steam vessel *Black Eagle* (which has the ladies on board and which tows us in front of the *Shearwater*).
8. The steam vessel *Lightning* . . . in front, which has gone to take our barge on board from the *Pique*.
9. The steam vessel *Fearless* (for survey).

This composes our squadron, besides which the Trinity House steamer goes with us, and, also, a packet. Innumerable little pleasure steamboats have been following us covered with people.

The voyage took nearly three days, travelling a total of 404 miles in 66 hours at an average speed of six knots. The Queen was less than pleased at being continually overtaken by a succession of coal-fired steamers. She also suffered sea-sickness during the trip, writing in her journal on the second day, 30 August: 'We heard, to our great distress, that we had only gone 58 miles since eight o'clock last night. How annoying and provoking this is! . . the sea was very rough towards evening, and I was very ill'. The next day was no better with The Queen recording: '. . . We heard, to our great vexation, that we had only been going three knots an hour in the night'.

But as the sea became calmer there were opportunities for a little relaxation, as Her Majesty wrote: 'The men begged leave to dance, which they did so to the sound of a violin played by a little sailor-boy; they also sang . . . We felt most thankful and happy that we were near our journey's end'.

The Queen was so annoyed at the performance of the *Royal George* that she refused to make the return journey in the Royal Yacht so a paddle steamer, *Trident*, was hired which, apparently was much more to Her Majesty's taste. So much so that when she arrived back in Windsor The Queen summoned the Prime Minister, Sir Robert Peel, to tell him that she was not prepared to suffer such indignities, and neither would she travel by sailing yacht again. So, without any of the Parliamentary debate and financial investigations that would accompany such a request today, the keel of the first steam Royal Yacht was laid down at Pembroke within three months.

The first *Victoria & Albert* was commissioned on 1 July 1843 under the command of Captain Lord Adolphus Fitzclarence. On her first visit to inspect the new yacht, which was being painted at the time, on 8 August 1843, Queen Victoria recorded in her journal: 'We drove from Woolwich to the Deptford Dockyard, where we inspected the *Victoria & Albert*, which is a beautiful vessel, with splendid accommodation'.

In August of that same year, The Queen and Prince Albert went on their first voyage in the new yacht, to visit King Louis Philippe of France at Eu. Her Majesty wrote to her uncle King Leopold I of the Belgians on 29 August, 'The yacht is quite delightful as to accommodation, & hitherto we have not even thought of being sick. Mais aujourd-'hui nous verrons'. The Queen's presentiments proved correct, and she recorded in her journal that 'towards one, it got very rough & we both began to feel very uncomfortable, so we went below. Considering how rough the sea was, I must say that the ship was very steady'.

During the 10 years of her life the *Victoria & Albert* was used on 20 occasions by Queen Victoria and Prince Albert, mainly to parts of the British Isles which in those days were largely inaccessible by road or even via the growing rail network. North Wales, the West Coast of Scotland, the Scilly Isles and in the yacht's first year alone, two visits to Europe, were all recorded in the ship's log. So the insistence by The Queen of having a new, steam-powered paddle yacht was already paying off.

Perhaps more surprising than any other aspect of the new Royal Yacht was the fact that The Queen obviously enjoyed travelling in her at all. She was a woman who disliked change in almost everything. She had been on the throne for five years before making that first voyage in the *Royal George* – and her unhappy experience caused some courtiers to feel that she might never set

When The Queen is ashore carrying out official engagements, her staff on board settle into a daily routine. The dressers, working from a schedule they have been given earlier, press and lay out the outfits Her Majesty will wear later that day. On a busy day The Queen can change clothes up to five times.

foot on board a ship again. But as with most innovations, The Queen, once she had been convinced, adopted them with remarkable enthusiasm. Throughout the rest of her reign she made great use of two of the three successive Royal Yachts she commissioned (the third was not used simply because Her Majesty had died before she was brought into full service). Smaller tenders were used to convey members of the Royal Family and the Household on shorter journeys and in shallow waters.

It was in 1846 when Queen Victoria bought Osborne House on the Isle of Wight as a private residence that the need for smaller, more economical vessels became apparent. The *Victoria & Albert* was far too large to be used simply as a ferry to and from the mainland so, to supplement *The Fairy*, the yacht's tender, a further craft, *The Elfin*, was built.

This was a workhorse in every sense of the word, carrying out what was described as 'the milk run' on a daily basis. By 1878 it had been refined into a well-worn routine which was described by the Yacht's temporary commander, Captain Watts: 'The duty of *The Elfin* was to leave Portsmouth, while The Queen was at Osborne, every weekday about 10 o'clock with the London papers and official correspondence for Osborne, landing them at Osborne Bay, and then proceeding to Cowes; leave Cowes at about 2 p.m. with The Queen's Messenger, taking him to Southampton with Government despatches, land him there and embark another, taking him to Cowes and remaining there until 7 a.m. the next day, when she proceeded to Portsmouth, to leave again at 10 a.m.'

It was during Queen Victoria's reign

The Elfin, a workhorse which did a daily 'milk run' between Portsmouth and the Isle of Wight, 1899. (Beken of Cowes)

that yacht racing became the fashionable sport it remains. Cowes Week, in August, was the focal point of high society, and in 1864, The Queen's eldest son, the Prince of Wales (later King Edward VII) competed in person for the first time. His presence revitalised this sport, as would, over 100 years later, the participation of his great-great-granddaughter, Princess Anne, in equestrian sports, by three-day eventing.

The 19th century Prince of Wales took part in yacht racing for the rest of his life, owning more than two dozen yachts, including one which became among the best-known racing yachts in the world – the *Britannia*. In a four-year period between 1893–97 *Britannia* won 157 prizes in 219 races. She was sold and bought back by the Prince (once when he was King) on two occasions –

the last one being in 1902.

King Edward took part in many races but he resisted the urge to handle the boat himself, preferring to sit in the stern wearing a panama hat and smoking a large cigar. When his son, George V, inherited *Britannia* he restored the yacht to its rightful place as the leading craft at many regattas, often taking the helm himself. King George V so loved *Britannia* that when he died in 1936 he left orders that she should be scuttled in the English Channel.

Her 50-ft boom was erected in the grounds of Carisbrooke Castle on the Isle of Wight as a flagstaff, her fittings were auctioned and raised £1,025 for King George V's Fund for Sailors, and her furniture and crockery were sent to Buckingham Palace. Then, with a garland of flowers over her bow, she was

With the ship's company at attention, the Royal paddle steamer Alberta *carries the sovereign during Cowes Week, 1899.* (Beken of Cowes)

The wheelhouse containing the wheel from one of Britannia's illustrious predecessors, the racing yacht, also named Britannia, *which won hundreds of prizes for King Edward VII and his son, King George V. The wheel is used to this day by the Yacht's helmsman.* (Courtesy H.M. Yacht)

towed by two Naval destroyers into the Channel where a party of sailors placed a charge of explosives on board. Within five minutes her remains had disappeared beneath the waves.

The present *Britannia* has a serviceable memento of her famous namesake: the wheel which guided that yacht to so many racing victories has been installed in the wheelhouse and is used to this day by the helmsman.

To return to the large State Yachts, it became apparent in the mid-19th century that a replacement would be needed for the *Victoria & Albert* which had become too slow and indeed small for the needs of The Queen and her growing family. Even The Queen had to agree that her yacht was getting past its best. On Monday, 16 August 1847 she wrote: '. . . Something had gone wrong with the paddle-wheel – just as happened last year – and it took full two hours to set it right'.

Even so it took some years for a replacement to be built. But in July 1855 the second *Victoria & Albert* was brought into service (originally her name was to be *Windsor Castle*). She was to prove the most successful of all three Royal Yachts in Victoria's time and by far the most popular with The Queen. Half as long again as her predecessor at 360-ft, she was four knots faster, with a much greater range. During the next 45 years she was to be used by members of the Royal Family more than 150 times with 100 of her voyages being to foreign ports.

When *Victoria & Albert II* was being built, Prince Albert involved himself in the design and decoration of the Royal Apartments, in much the same way as Prince Philip was to do a century later. The Prince Consort designed the gimbal table which today stands in the Drawing Room of *Britannia* – a brass counterweight beneath the table enables it to remain steady in all but the fiercest of gales.

Queen Victoria also made known her preferences in the furnishing and decoration of the yacht. She had never disguised her distaste for the ostentatious decor of the *Royal George* which had, in part, been carried over into the first

Victoria & Albert. In her new yacht she was determined that her apartments would be as near as possible a 'home from home'. So out went the gilt, rich brocades and fancy wood carving and in came the country house style of comparative simplicity and comfort that she and her husband preferred.

This is not to suggest that there was any compromise on luxury; far from it. The State Dining Room could seat up to 18 in comfort. The very best china, cutlery and crystal were used. Liveried footmen with powdered wigs (Prince Philip ended this latter requirement in the 1950s) attended every guest, while the floor was covered in a deep carpet of Royal crimson. Her Majesty's bedroom was similarly furnished and decorated. The walls were of highly polished bird's-eye maple, instead of the dark mahogany of earlier yachts, with a light airy theme of rosebud pattern chintz for the bed covers, the side chairs and the dressing table stool. The doors had ivory handles and the room contained electroplated fittings. Adjoining was a wardrobe room in which The Queen's

The State Dining Room on the Victoria & Albert II *where liveried footmen in powdered wigs attended the guests.* (© The Royal Collection 1995. HM The Queen)

dresser slept.

Immediately below The Queen's suite were 12 cabins for the Household, of which six were twin and, in line with the strict moral codes of the day, the cabins of the Ladies-in-Waiting were located along the starboard (right) side of the yacht while those of the Lords-in-Waiting were on the port (left) side.

The Dining Room featured an open fireplace alongside which stood a brass coal scuttle fashioned like a nautilus shell. In the Drawing Room, 26-ft by 18-ft 6-ins, there was an Erard piano, an oval centre table, two sofas and three easy chairs, with the whole floor being covered in an elegant Brussels carpet.

It was on the 12 July 1855 that The Queen and Prince Albert went for their first sail in *V&A II*. They spent an afternoon sailing off the Isle of Wight from Osborne and both were much impressed. The Queen wrote: '. . . it is indeed a most magnificent & enormous vessel. One feels quite lost in her!'

Five days later, on 17 July, they embarked for their visit to the Emperor Napoleon III, spending the first night

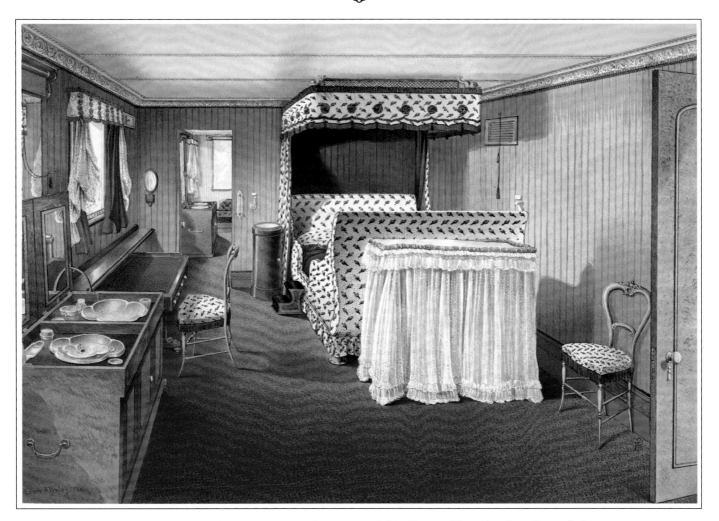

in 'this splendid ship, with a lovely view of dear Osborne from the windows of my sitting cabin', anchored off Osborne. The Queen recorded next day, 'Could not sleep at all for a long time, though the Yacht is most comfortable. At 5 we got under way. From the rapidity at which she goes, there is a good deal of vibration'.

SOUGHT SOLITUDE ON AFTER DECK

The Prince and Princess of Wales were frequent users of the yacht. Prince Edward often took guests for Mediterranean cruises in the summer months while the Princess remained in England.

But when Prince Albert died in 1861, Queen Victoria virtually ended her overseas travel and confined herself, on the occasions when she used the yacht, to short voyages around the coast of Britain. She would sit on the after-deck attended by one of her Indian servants who made sure that nobody interrupted the solitude The Queen wanted in widowhood.

It was in 1887, Jubilee Year, that The Queen had decided to engage a number of Indian servants and one of them, Abdul Karim, advanced to become The Queen's Indian Secretary, being known as the Munshi Hafiz Abdul Karim. The Munshi was in constant attendance. His devotion, silence, and ability to anticipate Her Majesty's every wish made him an admirable companion during the final years of her life, even if the Court

Queen Victoria's bedroom where the doors had ivory handles. Adjoining is the wardrobe room in which Her Majesty's dresser slept. (© The Royal Collection 1995. HM The Queen)

hated him and resented his influence.

A century ago the basic ground rules were laid which are still in effect on board the present Royal Yacht: no shouting, nobody approaches the Royal Apartments or the afterdeck unless in the course of duty, and The Queen is to be left alone at all times. This is presumably why today The Queen has often told friends that *Britannia* is the only place where she can truly relax. Even at Balmoral and Sandringham it is difficult for her to get away from everyone. Here she is left completely alone when she wants to be, and that is why she loves it so.

It was in 1888 that electric lights were first provided on board. The lamps and candelabra in the Dining Room, originally made to burn candles, were converted to electricity a few years later

Queen Victoria leaving after a stay at her beloved Osborne House on the Isle of Wight to return to the mainland, 1899. (Beken of Cowes)

on the orders of King Edward VII.

Queen Victoria made her final voyage in the Royal Yacht in 1900 when she sailed to Ireland. After 45 years of unbroken service the *Victoria & Albert II* was retired, though not without protest from The Queen, who regarded the yacht with particular favouritism as one of the places where she and her beloved husband had enjoyed so much relaxation. However, she was persuaded that the craft was outmoded and was fast being superseded by the yachts of her European relations, the Czar of Russia and the German Kaiser. This final argument convinced Her Majesty that Britain must remain in the vanguard of Royal transportation at sea – as elsewhere – and a new yacht, *Victoria & Albert III*, powered by massive steam engines driven through twin-screw

Another relic from bygone days. The 'Rum Tot' tub, used in Queen Victoria's time and which today stands — without the rum — in the Sun Lounge. (Courtesy H.M. Yacht)

propulsion, was launched at Pembroke in May 1899. Her cost was £510,034; equivalent to around £50 million at today's prices.

The Queen's reservations about the need for a new yacht proved to be correct, though accidental. The vessel nearly capsized at her launching due to faulty design and construction. This was in part because the builders had been given plans based on those used for the yacht of the Czar of Russia – and the ship's architects had neglected to check to see if the measurements were to European metric or British Imperial standards. Eventually all was corrected, at a cost of almost another half million pounds, but the fact remained that The Queen never once went on board her new yacht. She was, of course, becoming

old and feeble by the time that yacht was launched and had died by the time she was commissioned in July 1901.

On 22 January 1901, Queen Victoria died peacefully at Osborne. The honour of carrying her body back to the mainland from the Isle of Wight fell to her Royal Yacht tender, *Alberta*, built in 1865. It was a most impressive sight as eight destroyers led the floating cortege followed by *Victoria & Albert*, *Osborne* and *Hohenzollern*, the State Yacht of the Kaiser, with the Trinity House yacht *Enchantress* bringing up the rear. So King Edward VII began his reign as the proud possessor of a magnificent new Royal Yacht, the *Victoria & Albert III*. She was to serve four sovereigns before coming to the end of her career as a Royal Yacht in 1939. During the

King Edward VII began his reign as proud possessor of a brand new Royal Yacht, Victoria & Albert III *which was to serve four sovereigns before being broken up in 1955.*
(Reproduced by permission of Wright & Logan)

Second World War she was used as an accommodation ship in Portsmouth, before being broken up at Faslane in 1955.

The *Victoria & Albert III* was without doubt the most splendid of all three *V&As* though she did not find favour at first. In October 1900, the Prince of Wales (later Edward VII) described her as 'simply hideous, far too large & unwieldy & draws too much water'. A few weeks later he was prepared to modify his opinion to the extent of saying, 'I believe the new Royal Yacht is perfectly safe & she may be made comfortable, but I fear she will always be ugly'.

By the time he sailed in her, as King, to Germany for the funeral of his sister, the Empress Frederick, many improvements had been made. The King's Private Secretary reported, 'The King and Queen were very much pleased with the new Royal Yacht when they crossed in her to Flushing the other day. She certainly is most comfortable & luxurious & in these respects she beats the Russian & German Yachts. I think too that her

outward appearance has improved'.

The third *Victoria & Albert* had two yellow funnels, three masts, and her hull was painted a distinctive black and gold. She was constructed of steel covered with teak planking, had a range of 2,500 miles at 14 knots and, at 4,700 tons, she was the largest yacht in the world, burning 714 tons of coal. She carried a crew of 367 plus 40 Royal servants when The King was on board. She was 80-ft longer than her predecessor, her twin-screws made her faster, quieter and much more stable, and The King had stamped his own personality on her interior decoration and furnishing.

His Majesty loved to entertain lavishly on board. The Dining Room could seat 30 guests in comfort. Hepplewhite chairs were specially designed for the yacht and are used today in the State Dining Room in *Britannia* (the extra 26 chairs needed to bring the seating capacity up to its present 56 are identical copies of the originals).

The Dining Room was connected to a serving room where there was a hot-

plate and a food lift from the galley, two decks below. This meant that the food could be served hot, which had not always been the case in previous yachts. Royal Marines used to carry the food from the kitchens to the service lifts.

The decoration included two silver-gilt speaking trumpets and a silver telescope from the *Royal George*. The clock was of Wedgwood china and the sideboards were made of feathered satinwood.

This yacht was the first to have electricity installed throughout. One of Queen Alexandra's party pieces was to press a button beside her chair in the Dining Room after dinner to detonate two six-pound cannon just outside. On at least one occasion an elderly guest, said to be the Archbishop of Canterbury, was taken by complete surprise and nearly had a heart attack at this unconventional after-dinner entertainment. Queen Alexandra was practically stone deaf so the noise of the guns didn't bother her in the least, and The King, who knew what was coming, was always

highly amused at the reaction of their guests.

There was a Smoking Room with mahogany panelling, furnished in rich red morocco. A full-length mirror stood in the corridor outside The King's bedroom so that His Majesty could check his appearance, which was always immaculate, before meeting his guests.

The Queen's bedroom was carpeted in pale green, The King choosing Royal blue, and there were 14 cabins for guests, with a further seven for maids and valets.

Originally a separate Royal Household dining room had been planned. But The King decided that members of the Household would dine at the Royal table while on board, so their dining room was converted into three cabins: the first for three servants, the second for the Superintendent of Police, and the third to be used as a Post Office.

King Edward VII made extensive use of the yacht, sailing to many European ports, using the *V&A* as a floating

The majestic Victoria & Albert III, *commissioned in 1901 and used as the Royal Yacht until 1939. The ship behind her is the* Standardt, *the Russian Royal Yacht, 1909.* (Beken of Cowes)

palace. It was in every respect a ship of State. His Majesty was a charming if demanding host, and the food and wine served on board compared favourably, as it does to this day, with that served at any of the Royal residences ashore.

Dinner on board was always a formal affair. The gentlemen wore full evening dress – white tie, tails and decorations (it was to be many years before dinner jackets and black ties were considered acceptable). Ladies wore long evening dresses complete with diamonds, jewels and, as a former Master of the Household once remarked, 'every rock in the book'.

His Majesty was the perfect host and demanded equal standards in the behaviour of his guests. Woe betide anyone, male or female, who turned up late or wearing what The King regarded as the wrong outfit for the occasion. One confused diplomat arrived on board the *Victoria & Albert* in 1907 clad in what he thought was the correct uniform, full Court dress including knee breeches. He was despatched immediately by The King who informed him icily: 'trousers are always worn on board ship'.

His Majesty's dinners on board would usually include 12 courses, occasionally 15. They would start with oysters, perhaps a dozen or so, followed by soup with sherry, caviar, and several fish dishes. Then came the serious business of the evening, the main courses. There would be fowl, game, mutton, beef and lamb, all with lashings of fresh vegetables in rich creamy sauces. The King loved his puddings so several were offered, to be rounded off with ice-cream. The finest wines and champagnes were drunk during the meal – and for the guests there was only one problem.

Traditionally, The King would always be served first, and start as soon as the food was placed in front of him.

As he ate first he also finished before anyone else and as soon as his plate was removed so too were the plates of everyone else – whether they had finished or not! Consequently, there were occasions when some guests had scarcely taken their first mouthful before their plates were removed. Fortunately, this is one Royal tradition that has been allowed to lapse.

The King always took his own servants with him on board the Royal Yacht. He had 31 in all including an Arab boy whose sole duty was to provide His Majesty with a constant supply of his favourite coffee. He also invariably was accompanied by his little fox-terrier Caesar, a dog who, like some of The Queen's corgis today, took a delight in attacking everyone except his Royal master. Private Secretaries have long learned to ignore the attentions of the Royal dogs, at least while within sight of the Monarch. The occasional sly kick has been known to happen though when out of Royal eyesight.

King Edward VII brought Royal Yachts to the forefront of public attentions both at home and abroad during his nine years on the throne. He was a brilliant sportsman who loved all aspects of sailing and, both as Prince of Wales and King, enjoyed being at sea as often as he could. The crew of the Royal Yacht adored him and, although always aware of his own position, he managed to convey a feeling of shipboard 'esprit de corps' to all his Yachtsmen no matter what their rank.

When King George V came to the throne in 1910 he did not use the Royal Yacht to anything like the same extent as his father. He too was a sailor King with a great love of the sea, but this did not extend to foreign lands and certainly not to foreigners. Consequently, he did not travel abroad on State Visits using the Royal Yacht, nor did he entertain extensively on board. His attitude to sailing was that it was something to be done in small, fast craft, purely for sport.

As Prince of Wales he had used the yacht as transport when making official and private visits on the Continent such as when he, with the Princess of Wales, crossed the North Sea in the *Victoria & Albert* to attend the coronation at Trondheim of the King and Queen of Norway. And every summer the Royal Yacht was anchored off the Isle of Wight for Cowes Week which The King regularly attended. In 1913 he even interrupted his holiday to summon his Private Secretary Lord Stamfordham on board to discuss the Irish situation. Years later, in 1925, The King sailed in the *Victoria & Albert* on a Mediterranean cruise as part of his convalescence following a severe attack of influenza and bronchitis. But only after insisting that Lord Stamfordham warn all would-be hosts that he did not want to meet any of them. 'The King does not wish to see any French officials during his journey

through France' the Private Secretary told the British Ambassador in Paris.

The cruise was a success, mainly because The King was accompanied by The Queen and his favourite sister, Princess Victoria. Also because the captains of the two escorting warships were old friends who shared His Majesty's nautical sense of humour.

During the reign of King George V the *Victoria & Albert* ceased to occupy her previous position as the monarch's 'floating palace'. The King simply did not care to use her, or any other ship for that matter, for extensive overseas tours. But the *V&A* was used to carry His Majesty in the great Silver Jubilee Review of the Fleet in 1935. King Edward VIII did not use the yacht on any occasion but his brother, who succeeded him as King George VI, was very fond of the old craft and used her for his Coronation Review of the Fleet in 1937, and several times for ceremonial duties in home waters in the short period leading up to the Second World War. Perhaps the happiest occasion of all was when The King and Queen took their

HMS Surprise *was used as a Royal Yacht by The Queen for the Coronation Review of the Fleet in 1953, before* Britannia *was commissioned.* (Reproduced by permission of Wright & Logan)

two daughters, Princess Elizabeth and Princess Margaret, with them on the West Country cruise of 1939, shortly before the outbreak of hostilities. As they lay off Dartmouth a young cadet from the Royal Naval College came on board to dine and that was the first recorded meeting between Princess Elizabeth and Prince Philip.

By this time it was obvious that a replacement was urgently needed for the *Victoria & Albert*. A Cabinet meeting in July 1938 agreed that a new Royal Yacht should be built at a cost of £900,000 – with a proviso that in the event of war it should also be used as a hospital ship. This last condition was partly to prevent what the politicians feared could be a public outcry over the extravagance of the taxpayer being asked to pay for a yacht in a time of deep recession. As it happened the plans came to nothing as war was declared in September 1939 and the idea was shelved for the duration.

It was to be 14 years before a new Royal Yacht would appear. For the Coronation Review of the Fleet undertaken by Elizabeth II in 1953 a former frigate, *HMS Surprise*, was used. Later that same year when Her Majesty and the Duke of Edinburgh set sail for the Commonwealth Tour, a passenger liner, the *SS Gothic* was chartered from the Shaw Saville and Albion Line and specially adapted for Royal service. The charter cost was £40,000 a month. The Palace then had to foot the bill for painting the ship white, the colour decided on for the duration of the Royal tour, and afterwards for it to be repainted to its original black.

The need for a new Royal Yacht was now urgent.

BRITANNIA

IT WAS IN 1938 that the Admiralty had first considered the possibility of building a replacement for the *Victoria & Albert*. In 1939 outline drawings and plans for the essential requirements were drawn up and sent to the leading shipbuilders in Britain. The Second World War put a stop to the plans and it wasn't until 1951 that the idea was revived.

The Admiralty announced in October of that year that a medium-sized hospital ship was to be built with the dual role of acting as a Royal Yacht in peacetime. King George VI was in full agreement with the plans and at the planning stage he made many suggestions for reducing expenditure. Economy was the watchword throughout. When the final plans were submitted towards the end of 1951 they were approved by His Majesty, and subsequently further approved by The Queen, early in 1952, the first year of her reign.

The idea of a hospital ship was not just a sop to public opinion but a realistic approach to the problem of combining the needs of the Royal Navy with those of the Royal Family. Indeed, it was the requirements of the hospital ship which took precedence at that time. The Medical Director General of the Navy was involved in the earliest stages of the design, to make it possible to proceed with the construction of a hospital ship and a Royal Yacht concurrently.

Two hundred patients were to be accommodated in wards in the after part of the ship where the Royal Apartments were also to be located. Individual cubicles were to be erected in the Drawing Room, and tuberculosis patients requiring 'fresh-air' beds were to be housed on the Verandah Deck, with others occupying the space now used for Royal bedrooms. A dental surgery and laboratory were planned for the main deck. Below this were the operating theatre and anaesthetic rooms together with other specialist facilities such as a physiotherapy room, pathology laboratory and an X-ray department.

The plans included details of how

The Royal Marines Band rehearses in the morning and plays every evening during dinner. Their programme for official events has been chosen before leaving England, and also printed, so it is difficult to get anything changed. However, there is no advance programme for everyday informal occasions and the Director of Music has a free hand to vary the style and theme.

many medical staff would be needed: eight medical and dental officers, five nursing sisters and 47 male ratings. In the event of the yacht being used as a hospital ship in wartime, she would be manned by a Merchant Navy crew, sailing under a civilian flag, the Red Ensign, as opposed to the Royal Navy Yachtsmen who operate under the White Ensign, in normal conditions.

Part of the afterdeck was to be strengthened to enable helicopters to land and take-off. The ship's laundry was expanded to cope with the expected extra items that would be needed when the yacht was in her hospital ship configuration. This explains why the laundry on *Britannia* is very much larger than that required normally for a ship of her size.

All the suggested changes were incor-

porated in the original design and construction of the yacht. For 39 of her 42 years it has been feasible, if not very realistic, for *Britannia* to be converted into a hospital ship if required. But the needs of the modern navy have overtaken the facilities available on the yacht, and in 1992 it was finally decided that there was no point in keeping up the pretence of being able to use her in this capacity. Accordingly, the scheme was officially dropped. The Royal Yacht is just that – a yacht and nothing else.

Regarding the building of the new Royal Yacht, seven firms were invited to make suggestions. From this list it became clear that John Brown & Co. of Clydebank offered the best prospect of meeting the demanding requirements of the Admiralty – in particular, the delivery date, which had been decided as

When Britannia *was being planned for dual use as a Royal Yacht and a hospital ship, part of the afterdeck was to be strengthened to allow helicopters to land.* (Courtesy H.M. Yacht)

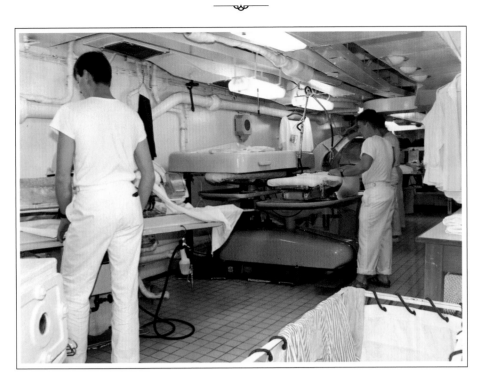

Britannia's laundry is larger than usual for a ship her size. This is because if she had been used as a hospital ship she would have needed the extra capacity. (Courtesy H.M. Yacht)

being the end of 1953 or the beginning of 1954 at the latest.

The contract was signed on 6 February 1952, just one day before King George VI died and his daughter became Elizabeth II. John Brown & Co. had an enviable record in shipbuilding, having been responsible for the giant liners *Queen Elizabeth* and *Queen Mary*. Years later they would also build what has been described as the last of the great liners – *Queen Elizabeth 2*.

From the outset the young Queen took a personal interest in every aspect of her new yacht. One of the first audiences of her new reign was granted to the Controller of Navy Construction on 29 February 1952, to discuss the project. Her Majesty instructed the Controller that she wished to meet the architect responsible to discuss the decorative scheme of the Royal Apartments.

Once the contract had been signed, one of the first appointments made was that of Mr J. Patrick McBride of McInnes Gardner & Partners of Glasgow to oversee the decoration of the State Apartments and the Royal suites. Mr McBride was one of the most experienced ships' architects in the world, having been frequently employed by John Brown in that capacity. He also knew something of The Queen's tastes as he had decorated the Royal Apartments on the *SS Gothic* for the forthcoming Commonwealth Tour. Her Majesty approved the appointment and received Mr McBride at Clarence House in July 1952 for the first of many informal discussions. He received a fixed fee of £2,400 for his services.

Over the next few months Mr McBride submitted various decorative schemes to the Palace and discussed them personally with The Queen and the Duke of Edinburgh. In March of the following year they expressed their pleasure at his work but asked him if, in view of the importance of the project, he would have any objection to their consulting other specialists in the field of decorative art on the proposals he had put forward. Naturally Mr McBride, no matter what his real feelings may have been, agreed to this suggestion, and

Prince Philip called in Gordon Russel of the Royal Society of Arts and the Council of Industrial Design. These were both organisations in which The Queen was interested, and following the meeting with Mr Russel, the proposal was made to appoint Sir Hugh Casson as Consultant Architect.

The Admiralty were not entirely enthusiastic about this idea and the Under Secretary of Finance recorded in a Minute of a meeting held on 21 March 1953:

a) Can Director of Naval Contracts say whether the proposed employment of Sir Hugh Casson, plus Mr McBride, is likely to increase the total cost of the Royal Yacht, as the situation is seen at present.

b) Can DNC be sure of being able to keep Sir Hugh Casson's and Mr McBride's projects under financial control, so that projects they might have in mind can be decided by the Admiralty . . . We particularly do not want a repetition of the activities of Miss Brigden in the *Gothic*, or a situation in which the Decorating Consultant/Consultants can submit possibly costly projects to the Palace, obtain Palace approval, and so commit the Admiralty.

(Miss Brigden had been employed as an extra consultant when the *Gothic* was being prepared for the Royal Tour. Several times she by-passed the Admiralty, obtaining Palace approval for certain schemes for which the Admiralty then had to find the money.)

Sir Hugh Casson was informally sounded out by the Duke of Edinburgh to see if he was willing to take on the job – and, of course, he said he would be delighted. The Admiralty then formally approached him. The Under Secretary for Finance, Mr P. N. N. Synnott, noted on 24 March 1953: 'In the circumstances, no financial objection is seen to this proposal. If Sir Hugh Casson asks for more than £250 – which it is hoped he will not – we will have to consult the Treasury'.

All this over an item which was costing less than one mirror in The Queen's Sitting Room.

This constant supervision of the costs involved in building *Britannia* continued throughout the construction, with volumes of correspondence on the tiniest detail. Sir Hugh Casson's final bill would amount to 700 guineas – for a project which meant he had to travel from London to Glasgow at least half a dozen times in the course of several months. His expenses, originally expected to amount to less than £50, finally added up to £184. But to obtain approval – and receive his cheque – he had to submit itemized expense accounts and write several times asking 'for something on account in order to pay my suppliers'.

The original estimate by John Brown's for the total cost of decorating the Royal Apartments was £55,000–£60,000. That was considered to be reasonable in view of the fact that had the quarters been decorated just to normal Ward Room standards the cost would have been £25,000. As it happened, by the time the final invoices

Britannia is of course the perfect choice for a honeymoon. Everyone on board knows that The Queen and her family value their privacy greatly and so they perform their duties as silently and quickly as possible. They are there if needed, 24 hours a day. When they are not required they keep well out of the way.

were submitted the cost had risen to £78,000. This included such additional items as a decorative mirror for The Queen's sitting room at £315, an embroidered panel for the headboard in Her Majesty's bedroom at £450, and a plaque bearing the Royal Coat of Arms which cost £400 in material plus £50 in labour charges.

But the extras were not all for the Royal Apartments. The Admiral commanding the Yacht was also allocated additional comforts over and above those normally afforded a ship's captain in the Royal Navy. There is one item listed under Group D of the extras raised by the builders which says: 'Admiral's Accommodation – Wood lining, ceiling and furniture in lieu of Admiralty Supply Steel furniture and painted steelwork; also special electrical fittings: £1,120 in materials and a further £845 in labour costs'.

One of the more distinctive characteristics of *Britannia* is the single gold line painted around her hull. The paint really is gold leaf and the original cost was £332. This has since escalated as the line has to be repainted every time the yacht has a refit.

The idea for the gold line came from The Queen herself, as did the colour for the hull. Traditionally, Royal Yachts were painted black, *Britannia*'s three immediate predecessors had black hulls, but Her Majesty decided that blue would be a more appropriate colour for her own yacht and so *Britannia* remains

The gold line around Britannia's *hull is one of her most distinctive characteristics and the idea came from The Queen herself, as did the colour of the yacht. All other Royal Yachts had been black, but Her Majesty decided that blue was the right colour for her yacht and* Britannia *is the only ship in the world with this shade.* (Courtesy H.M. Yacht)

Visitors often ask if there is more than one engine room, because this one looks like a showpiece. But this is it, with the original engines 42 years old and still going strong. (Courtesy H.M. Yacht)

the only ship in the world with this distinctive shade.

There was one item which could not be foreseen when the original plans were being drawn, but which had to be included as soon as the problem was discovered. It concerned the modesty of the Royal ladies. During tests it was found that the breeze circulating around the deck outside the fore end of the Royal Charthouse caused skirts to lift in a rather revealing manner, particularly to any eyes looking out from the bridge.

This obviously had to be rectified before The Queen and her family came on board so a teak bulwark was added as a modesty panel at a cost of £299. It is thanks to many tests carried out with

Central control – the bridge from which the Yacht's Commander oversees every movement of his Royal charge. (Courtesy H.M. Yacht)

Britannia *flying five standards: the Royal Standard, the flag of the Lord High Admiral (The Queen), two Union flags, and the White Ensign of the Royal Navy.*

Dressed overall, with all standards flying, Britannia *is saluted by a squadron of Royal Navy helicopters during the Spithead Review of 1977. (Courtesy of the Broadlands Archives)*

office girls wearing a variety of dresses, that now the Royal ladies can stand on the foredeck safe in the knowledge that naval courtesy has come to their aid – and there is no chance of a glimpse of Royal thigh!

Because *Britannia* was destined to be used as a floating palace and ship of State it was necessary for her to be fitted out with three masts (as were the *Victoria & Albert II* and *III*): The Main Mast, in the centre (139-ft 3-in), from which is flown the Royal Standard; the Fore Mast (133-ft) from which the flag of the Lord High Admiral (The Queen) is flown when Her Majesty is on board – this flag shows a yellow anchor lying on its side set against a red background – and the Mizzen Mast (118-ft 10-in) carrying the Union flag.

And as *Britannia* was going to be used not only for long distance transoceanic voyages, but also trips up-river in certain countries where a number of bridges would have to be negotiated, the top 20-ft of the Main Mast and the radio aerial on the foremast were hinged. The first time this happened

was in 1959 when *Britannia* sailed up the St. Lawrence Seaway which was opened by The Queen that year. The nautical term for the hinging manoeu-

At New York's busy sea front, Britannia *ties up near another of the city's nautical attractions, the giant aircraft carrier* USS Intrepid.

vre is 'scandalising'. One of the most unusual orders a Commander has ever had to give on board *Britannia* is when he shouted for the first time, 'Prepare to scandalise!'

The original estimate for the new Royal Yacht amounted to £1,615,000 including £290,000 profit. Eventually, the final price was £2,098,000 – possibly the best bargain this century.

THE PRIVATE NAVY

H.M.Y. BRITANNIA

FOR A SHIP of comparatively small size – *Britannia* is nearly 6,000 tons – the Royal Yacht appears at first to be excessively overmanned. There are 19 Officers and 217 Yachtsmen on board, (reduced from 277 as an economy measure).

The man in overall charge is Commodore Anthony Morrow, the first officer below the rank of Rear-Admiral to command the Royal Yacht. He succeeded Rear-Admiral Sir Robert Woodard in April 1995 and will have the distinction of being *Britannia*'s last Commander – until she is decommissioned in 1997. It was Admiral Woodard who coined the phrase 'My Private Navy' as a way of describing *Britannia*'s crew.

His full title was Flag Officer Royal Yachts, or FORY, which meant that, in theory, he controlled all the yachts used by the Royal Family. In previous reigns, where the Monarch frequently had a number of yachts, the Commander of *the* Royal Yacht also looked after the others, including racing yachts and sailing dinghies. During the present reign, for all practical purposes *Britannia* has been the sole responsibility. And with the appointment of Commodore Morrow, the description FORY has been allowed to lapse.

The title first came into use on 29 October 1951. Less than a month later King George VI approved the appointment of Admiral Lambe as his first FORY. The financial responsibilities of the Flag Officer were among the first rules to be laid down by the Lords of the Admiralty, particularly the expenses relating to the victualling of the Royal Household when its members were embarked. It was agreed that the Civil List would account for all such expenses 'excluding the cost of wine in the General Salon, which is to be paid by the individual giving the order'. The Civil List also pays for all entertainment given in The Queen's name, even when she is not present.

It is well known that *Britannia* was, until recently, the only ship in the world

Towards the end of most cruises the crew and members of the Household stage a concert attended by the Royal Family. A lot of preparation goes into the show which usually makes up in enthusiasm what it may lack in quality. The performers take this quite seriously, making sure their make-up and costumes are perfect, and several rehearsals are held on the fo'c'sle before the big night.

Commodore Anthony Morrow who took over as Commander of the Royal Yacht in South Africa in April 1995 and who will remain in command until she decommissions in 1997.

to have an Admiral in command, but why should this ever have been necessary? Was it simply to reflect the importance of the position in relation to the Crown? Would a mere four-ring Captain be considered too junior to command The Queen's personal Yacht, even if he had formerly run, say, an aircraft carrier or a nuclear submarine?

Admiral Woodard has his own viewpoint, explaining that as the Yacht is an independent command, answerable only to Her Majesty, he did not work through the Royal Navy, other than to obtain resources. His rank was important as a reflection of the responsibilities of his command. And even though his money came from the Headquarters Budget of the Commander-in-Chief, he did not get his orders from him. Admiral Woodard told him where the Yacht was going and when, but there was no question of asking his permission.

There was also one other very practical reason for having an Admiral in charge. FORY liaises a great deal with officials from government departments at home and overseas. In certain countries they are more conscious of rank than in Britain and being an Admiral sometimes smoothed the path a little. The job carried with it a high profile and a type of ambassadorial role; there was an occasion when Admiral Woodard had to call on the President and Prime Minister of the Dominican Republic to express his happiness at arriving there to hold The Queen's official birthday party. It might have been considered a slight if a mere Commander had been produced instead of an Admiral and in certain circumstances it could be difficult to get in to see the right people. He had to fight his own corner to obtain, and keep, many of the items *Britannia* required – having two stars on his sleeve certainly helped.

It will be interesting to see the reaction when *Britannia* sails into foreign ports in the future. Particularly so where the host country always provides an escort and where – in for example, Australia, New Zealand, Canada or the United States – the Yacht's commander invariably has to deal with an Admiral.

Of course, this is no reflection on the new Commodore. He is an officer of wide experience in command, who has already served on the Royal Yacht on two previous occasions (1965–66 as Royal Barge Officer, and 1976–78 as Communications and Royal Cypher Officer). But it does seem to many people, both in the Royal Navy and else-

Members of the Permanent Royal Yacht Service (PRYS) who can choose to serve almost their entire Royal Navy careers in Britannia.

where, that the downgrading, which will mean a saving of just £7,000 a year, is an unnecessary adjustment at this stage of *Britannia's* long and distinguished life.

Everyone else serving on the Royal Yacht is chosen after an interview, with the officers being personally selected by the Commanding Officer. One of his senior officers will see every sailor who applies for Royal Yacht service.

In the old days there was no permanent crew on board the Royal Yachts. The officers came from other ships in the fleet, as required, and the Yachtsmen were employed as riggers in Portsmouth Dockyard when they were not needed for Royal service. Today there is something called the Permanent Royal Yacht Service, an elite corps of sailors who can choose to serve almost their entire naval career in the Royal Yacht. But this applies only to non-commissioned ranks; officers cannot join.

Britannia's crew is divided into two: the Permanent Royal Yacht Service (PRYS) and the Ocean Complement. This latter group consists of around 50 men who are employed on board only when the Yacht goes to sea. They work as additional engineers and deckhands, and it is from this group that the PRYS recruits its members. The PRYS is limited to around 190 and they are all volunteers. Once a man has served in the Ocean Complement for a year he is allowed to apply for the PRYS, as long as he has more than three years of his engagement to serve. Once in the PRYS it is very rare for anyone to leave before he reaches retirement age.

One of the Yacht's previous Coxswains, Warrant Officer Tatlow, who was known as 'Mister Yacht', had been on board for more than 25 years before retiring in 1992. Joining as an ordinary seaman, the lowest substantive rank in the Royal Navy, he became one

King Juan Carlos was so excited at the prospect of The Queen coming to his beloved Majorca, where he has a Summer Palace at Marevent, that he could not wait for the protocol to be observed. He just turned up having flown over from Barcelona the previous night.

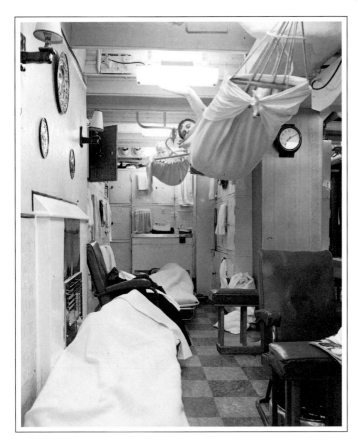

similar to that held in the Army by a Regimental Sergeant Major.

Warrant Officer Tatlow remembers when the crew slept in hammocks. When he first joined *Britannia* there were several sailors in his mess who had never slept in a proper bed – and never wanted to. 'Hammocks were wonderful to sleep in. The only problem was when you went ashore and had a couple of beers too many. When you came back and tried to climb in it could be a bit difficult, but most of us liked them and we were sorry to see them go.'

In those days the messes for the lower ranks contained up to 45 men and they literally lived in the space they were allocated. They slept in the hammocks and ate at tables just below. There were occasions when tempers became a bit frayed because of the confined space.

Eventually, after a refit in 1970, the hammocks were done away with and replaced by conventional bunks, but one man, Leading Seaman Jamie Stewart, who had never used an ordinary bed,

Conditions below deck before the major refit in 1970. Britannia was the last ship in the British Navy in which sailors slept in hammocks. (Courtesy of the late Sir Hugh Janion)

Living quarters for the 'Yotties' were slightly cramped and more than slightly spartan in the old days. (Courtesy of the late Sir Hugh Janion)

of the most influential people on board and frequently the senior officers would look to him for guidance. It is a position

It was considered to be a vast improvement when bunks replaced the hammocks, but there were still several Yachtsmen who said they could never get used to a proper bed. (Courtesy of the late Sir Hugh Janion)

turned down the chance every time, preferring to remain as he is.

When ratings are accepted into the Royal Yacht they are given a handbook which lays down the rules and regulations governing Royal Yacht Service. Particular emphasis is laid on dress. They are reminded that the 'Royal Yacht' cap ribbon makes them marked men ashore, so nothing but the highest standard is accepted. Royal Yachtsmen are also easily identified ashore when they are in civilian clothes. Even in the hottest climates they are required to wear collars and ties after 6.30 p.m. As one of the Yachtsmen said, 'You might be sweltering in South America or Singapore where everyone else is wearing shorts and T-shirts, but we have to stick to ties so we are easily picked out, and in an age where terrorist attacks are a constant threat it does seem a bit

This was when you found out who your friends were. If you didn't like your ship mates – hard luck! (Courtesy of the late Sir Hugh Janion)

was given special permission to keep his hammock. He carved his own niche in maritime history by becoming the last sailor in the British Navy to sleep in the way that sailors did back in Nelson's time.

There are few obvious advantages in serving in the Permanent Royal Yacht Service. The men do not receive any extra pay or allowances and there is one serious disadvantage: slow promotion. The only way to advance in *Britannia* is to fill 'dead men's shoes'. Because of this there are many men of vast experience and long years of service in the Navy who hold comparatively junior rank, simply because they have chosen to remain on the Yacht. One example is the Senior Petty Officer cook in the Ward Room Galley. He has had the opportunity a number of times of leaving the Yacht and being promoted to Chief Petty Officer, which would also mean a significant pay rise. But he has

Later there were separate quarters for eating, sleeping and relaxing. But even below decks, the Yachtsmen wear the regulation soft-soled shoes. (Courtesy of the late Sir Hugh Janion)

ridiculous to mark us out in this way'.

Another rule in the handbook states: 'As they mark the decks, shoes with black rubber soles or heels are not allowed on board'. The men are issued with soft-soled rubber plimsoles which are worn at all times to comply with the need for silence on the upper decks.

Traditions of dress on board the Royal Yacht are also strict. For example Yachtsmen must wear their uniform jumper inside the top of the trousers (all other sailors wear their jumpers outside). The reason for this exception is that a black silk bow is worn behind the trousers – a custom which came into being when Prince Albert died in 1861. Queen Victoria ordered the black bows to be worn as a mark of respect to her late husband, and her successors have

continued the tradition. One other distinction is that the Yachtsmen wear white badges instead of the red which are customary in the rest of the Navy.

They are also told that when the Yacht is on Royal Duty, caps are not worn if going anywhere aft of the Main Mast, in other words, near the Royal Apartments. This is to remove the need to salute members of the Royal Family whenever they are seen. This rule was encouraged by The Queen when the Duke of Edinburgh first urged it – both to save the Royal Family from constant salutes and the crew from always having to pay this courtesy. What happens when a Yachtsman meets one of the Royals is that he stands still until they have passed and speaks only if he has been acknowledged first, exactly the

same system that applies throughout the Royal Household ashore.

Smoking is allowed below decks on the Royal Yacht but not on the Upper Decks during working hours when a Standard is flying, either at sea or in harbour. Neither is smoking permitted when the Yacht is alongside in port

Dress at a formal function on board Britannia *depends on the climate. In the tropics evening wear is a thin dinner jacket with decorations for civilians. Naval officers wear white mess dress: black trousers, short white 'monkey' jacket, and black tie. Ladies always wear full length evening dresses and The Queen and other ladies in the Royal Family wear tiaras.*

away from Portsmouth if she is on Royal Duty.

If The Queen or any other member of the Royal Family is on board, all work that needs to be done aft of the Main Mast i.e. near the Royal Apartments, has to be finished by 9 a.m. After this the men are allowed into this area only if they are on duty. If, for example, the Signalman needs to go on to the Quarter Deck after this time he must use the 'underground route' – the main and lower deck passages, and not the upper deck.

One of the privileges the Yachtsmen do enjoy is being able to bring their families and friends on board when the Yacht is not on Royal Duty. The only exception is if the friend happens to be a journalist. The Press are not allowed on

The Yachtsmen's mess, bright and airy, where the food is served cafeteria style and there is plenty of elbow room for everyone. (Courtesy of the late Sir Hugh Janion)

board except for professional reasons – then, their visits are carefully supervised by the Admiral's Secretary, who is always a Commander, or by special arrangement with The Queen's Press Secretary. Yachtsmen are also warned never to speak to the media when they are ashore. They are allowed to have a camera on board with the written permission of the Commander, but no photography is allowed when the Royal Family is on board, and guests are forbidden to bring cameras with them.

There is also a Royal Marines contingent on board who live in a separate mess of their own called the 'Barracks'. They are incorporated into the Royal Yacht as fully paid up Yachtsmen and come under the direction of a sergeant. Traditionally there has always been a certain amount of rivalry between Royal Marines and sailors in the Royal Navy, but in *Britannia* there seems to be a genuine *esprit de corps* that includes both ser-

The Petty Officers Mess with a bar that could grace any hotel. An invitation to have a drink here is highly sought after by Buckingham Palace staff when they are on board.
(Courtesy of the late Sir Hugh Janion)

The Queen likes to meet the families of her Yachtsmen. Here she receives flowers from little Stuart Hunt, the son of Britannia's *official photographer, at the start of the Western Isles cruise.*
(Courtesy H.M. Yacht)

The Royal Marines contingent lives in a separate mess on board called 'the Barracks'. As well as providing sentries they also mix in with the rest of the crew, standing watch and helping to load stores. (Courtesy H.M. Yacht)

vices. The Marines carry out security duties and provide sentries when the Royal Family are embarked, but at all other times they mix in with the rest of the crew, carrying out watch duties and helping in loading stores, moving furniture on Sea Days and generally acting in exactly the same way as the rest of the Yachtsmen.

A Royal Marines Band is also embarked for all major tours and whenever a Sea Day is planned, either in a British port or abroad. The Band consists of a Director of Music and 26 musicians all drawn from the Band of the Commander-in-Chief, Naval Home Command. Their Director of Music (DOM) is a commissioned officer who lives in *Britannia*'s Ward Room but he probably spends more time with his men than is usual with other officers on board. The Band rehearses every morning in a mess-room in the for'ard end of the Yacht and their rehearsal time is

The Royal Yacht's crew gather on the foredeck for the traditional 'crossing the line' ceremony. (Courtesy of the Broadlands Archives)

London's Canary Wharf is the setting for this evening entertainment provided by the Royal Marines Band.

strictly controlled so that too much noise is avoided.

Whenever *Britannia* leaves or arrives in port the Band parades on deck and plays. One of the highlights of any evening's entertainment given by The Queen is the ceremony of Beat Retreat when the Band marches and counter-

marches on the quayside in a programme lasting around 25 minutes.

In 1984 when *Britannia* was in Southern California, The Queen gave a special dinner party on board to celebrate the wedding anniversary of President and Mrs Ronald Reagan. The President had been a film actor before entering politics and thought he had seen every side of show business. However, at the end of the evening, when Beat Retreat had been completed, he turned to Her Majesty and said, 'I thought Hollywood was the entertainment capital of the world, but there's no way we could beat this'.

The function of the Band is mainly orchestral, playing indoors at functions given by The Queen on board. But as all the musicians are able to play wind instruments as well, it is a simple matter to transform the Band into a ceremonial marching band or a concert military ensemble for a variety of outdoor occasions. The members of the Band also form themselves into smaller groups for dances, cocktail parties or receptions, while the pianist occasionally plays the Drawing Room piano for guests in the evening.

Unlike most other service units, the Royal Marines Band on board *Britannia* is permitted to undertake outside engagements on a commercial basis. The DOM acts as the Band's manager and he will quote for anything from a trio to a full-scale orchestra. They have a three-hour programme for the full Band which anyone can hire for around £3,000, or there's a smaller, five-piece group available at around £800 for the evening.

The Royal Navy is aware of this little bit of private enterprise and even

The Petty Officer cook in the main galley could have moved on many times and been promoted but he prefers life on Britannia *and is content to remain in his present rank.* (Courtesy H.M. Yacht)

encourages it, saying it advertises the standard of musicianship in the Royal Marines. The players themselves love the idea of performing outside – and, of course, the extra money, which they are allowed to keep.

The Band is probably the only group on board who do not always relish the idea of long voyages. Being away from Britain for too long means they lose the chance of lucrative 'gigs' ashore.

The Director of Music has a longer tour of duty than most other officers on the Royal Yacht. He serves for up to four years, whereas officers are normally appointed for two years. The Commanding Officer normally stays for five years, while the Keeper and Steward of the Royal Apartments, who is a Lieutenant Commander, can remain in the job even longer. This is because of his unique knowledge of the requirements of the Royal Family and their

One of the Season Officer's tasks is to help arrange sporting fixtures for Britannia's various teams.

preference for seeing familiar faces around them when they come on board.

25 ROYAL STAFF FOR STATE TRIP

Included in the 21 officers appointed to the Royal Yacht for two years are three officers known as Season Officers. These appointments date back to the days when the Royal Yachts were used only in the summer months and tied up alongside the dockyard in the winter. Extra officers were then needed for Cowes Week and the rest of the summer cruises.

The three Season Officers are the most junior in the Yacht and if there is a particularly boring or unpleasant job that needs to be done by an officer, you can be sure the cry will be, 'Send for a Season. He'll do it – it's good for him!' They live in the most cramped cabin flat

in the Yacht, in a section that's known as The Ghetto, but as they are invariably young men, they adapt to the conditions very well and most of them say they thoroughly enjoy their year in *Britannia*.

One of the Season Officers is allocated the duties of being Household Liaison Officer. This rather grand title disguises the fact that he is really a 'fixer' for the Staff of the Royal Household when they come on board. He doesn't deal with the senior Members of the Household and Officials; that's left to the Admiral and Keeper and Steward.

During the time when *Britannia* is in her home base of Portsmouth the Household Liaison Officer travels up to Buckingham Palace before each cruise to find out what the Travelling Yeoman in the Master of the Household's office wants him to arrange in the coming weeks.

With up to 25 Royal servants on board for a full State Visit there's plenty to keep him busy, looking after the transport arrangements when social and sporting functions are planned, and trying to sort out some of the countless problems that arise when so many people with different requirements demand your attention.

The current Household Liaison Officer says one problem he encountered came about when he had to make separate transport arrangements for The Queen's dressers. Most of the staff live below decks in cabins allocated to them by the Master of the Household, but the dressers, who are very much The Queen's personal staff, live on the Shelter deck alongside the Royal bedrooms. They do not venture into the nether regions occupied by their colleagues, so when the HLO posts a notice telling the staff of the programme he

Off-duty activities range from soccer, cricket and swimming to the more esoteric — there's even a Morris Dancing group on board.

The nearest that most people ever get to Britannia is when they are allowed within hailing distance. Here a party of sightseers hope for a glimpse of a Royal face just off Pitcairn Island. (Courtesy of the Broadlands Archives)

has arranged for them the dressers do not always see it. He then has to make sure they know what is on offer and find out if they want to join in.

Transport is another of his duties. While the staff travel in buses to and from the Yacht, the dressers require a car as they carry The Queen's personal valuables, and it is the HLO's responsibility to make sure this is always organised.

There is a lot of competition to be selected as an officer on the Royal Yacht as it is regarded as a showpiece ship where the Royal Navy itself is on display to The Queen. Therefore it follows that it is very much in the Navy's interests to put its best men forward so that Her Majesty will see the highest standards. The calibre of the officers can be gauged by the fact that many of the Royal Navy's most senior officers today,

and in the past, served in the Royal Yacht as junior lieutenants. A two-year stint in *Britannia* can be a great career boost to an ambitious young mariner.

During the last century the number of admirals who started their climb to the top from the decks of a Royal Yacht runs well into double figures. Perhaps the most famous of all former Royal Yacht officers was Prince Louis of Battenberg (later 1st Marquess of Milford Haven and father of Earl Mountbatten of Burma). He served on both the *Osborne* and *Victoria & Albert* in Queen Victoria's reign, and went on to become First Sea Lord, the most powerful man in the Royal Navy, during the reign of King George V.

At one time it was considered commonplace for officers to lobby influential figures at Court and at the

Admiralty in order to obtain a posting to the Royal Yacht, and it was even possible to buy a place. Queen Victoria put a stop to this practice, saying she thought it was unseemly for her officers to be seen bargaining in such a fashion. But she did not get rid of any of her officers who had obtained their positions in this way; there was even one occasion when the then captain of her yacht (later Admiral Lord Beresford) suggested that it might be in Her Majesty's interests for officers on the Royal Yacht to be rotated. She would have none of it saying, 'I like familiar faces around me, I don't want any changes'.

Strangely, *Britannia* is the only Royal residence nowadays in which the senior personnel do change frequently. The Royal Family today still like to see the same faces around them wherever they are, which is, presumably, one of the reasons why the Permanent Royal Yacht Service came into being. And the man who is closest of all to The Queen and her family when they are on board, the Keeper and Steward of the Royal Apartments, remains in the post for years on end – usually until he retires from the Navy. But, surprisingly, the other officers have to leave after their two-year tour is ended so there is a large turnover of officers who serve and have served on the Royal Yacht.

One of the first things an officer has to learn when he is posted to *Britannia* is the Christian name of every member of his division and those of the crew with whom he comes into contact. The Royal Yacht is unique in that all the Yachtsmen are called by their first names, or nicknames, by the officers. Nobody is quite sure how this custom started but it contributes to the overall impression of quiet informality on board, even if it does mean that newcomers have to do rather a lot of home-work – a bit like the Speaker in the House of Commons – so that they can put the right names to over 200 faces.

Life on board is comfortable for officers. Their cabins are single, small but adequate, while the Ward Room serves the most delicious food and excellent wine.

There is a lot of official entertaining on *Britannia* which means the mess bills can be high, but as these are deducted from the officers' pay before they see it, it is not quite as painful as having to sign large cheques at the end of each month.

When *Britannia* is in port, even when there is no member of the Royal Family on board, the officers dine in black tie; the best silver, china and cutlery are used and every dinner takes on a feeling of being a special occasion.

When Royalty is embarked the officers are informed what the senior Royal male member of the party will be wearing and they mirror those rigs, so that if one of them is summoned to join the Royal party at the last moment, as sometimes happens, they know they will be correctly dressed.

The Queen does not make a regular habit of asking her officers to join her for meals; her Ladies-in-Waiting and Private Secretaries usually dine with the family and the Commodore is in attendance. As far as the other officers are concerned it's a question of being ready to go when asked – an exception rather

Moving through the solid steel doors that divide the naval end from the yacht end is to enter another world. The bustle of everyday life below decks is replaced by a calm, dignified atmosphere in which it is not in the least bit difficult to imagine one is in a Royal residence.

Nowhere on her hull will you see her name, yet Britannia *is the most easily recognised ship afloat.* (Beken of Cowes)

than a rule. However they are invited to dine 'aft' once during the Western Isles cruise in the summer.

Because *Britannia* travels to so many different foreign ports carrying the Sovereign as well as other members of the Royal Family, it follows that the officers are involved in a wide variety of social events. Hosts vie with each other to invite men from the Royal Yacht to join them at cocktail parties, dinners and receptions, hoping perhaps that a little of the Royal glamour will rub off. It also means that with *Britannia* being a showcase for the finest the Navy can offer, the officers need to have qualities over and above merely being excellent at their jobs.

When visitors first go on board and meet the Commodore and his officers it soon becomes apparent that the selection process has involved more than the usual trawl for engineers, navigators and seamen officers. The officers need that little extra something that makes them stand out in any crowd. They are all pastmasters at the art of conversation – equally at home making small-talk with middle-aged matrons in Plymouth, Japanese tycoons who have flown in from Tokyo just for one of the Sea Days, or with an Ambassador, Foreign Secretary or President who has to be entertained for anything from a few minutes to an entire evening.

The Navy must have a secret stock of young, amusing officers with innate good manners, impeccable breeding and first-class minds, who can engage enthusiastically in conversations about subjects in which they may have little interest, with people they have never met before, will probably never meet again, and with whom they have nothing whatsoever in common.

The present Royal Yacht has no female crew members and there are no plans to recruit any at the present time. The reasons given are that no suitable accommodation is available and additional showers and lavatories would have to be built. It is also pointed out that there is no precedent for having women on board. However, as far back as 1847 the Admiralty did authorise the appointment of a Stewardess of the Royal Apartments and that she should be paid as a Petty Officer – but not called one!

That first Stewardess was a Mrs Jane Hooper. She remained on board the *Victoria & Albert* for more than 30 years, even, in 1881, being recommended for a Long Service Medal. Unfortunately she didn't get her award because the Lords of the Admiralty said once again, 'there is no precedent'.

With four Commanders on board it might seem that the Commodore is little more than a figurehead; a superfluous character who is there simply to satisfy Royal protocol and to parade in full ceremonial uniform, dripping with gold braid, whenever *Britannia* is on show. Closer inspection reveals that he is a seaman with a long and distinguished career and that he has been chosen for this job because of his vast experience in a variety of posts.

Even though there are ceremonial and public duties to be carried out, his main function is to see that the Royal Yacht is able to perform her role in all winds and weathers; that she is capable of living up to her reputation both as the showcase of the Royal Navy and as a sea-going Royal residence. The day-to-day running of the Yacht is left in the capable hands of the Executive Officer, the senior of the four Commanders, but whenever *Britannia* leaves or enters port, Commodore Morrow is on the bridge, issuing orders and taking complete command of the Yacht.

In the left hand corner of the Drawing Room as you enter is a Walmar baby grand piano. This is fastened to the floor by bolts, in case it might take off in bad weather.

The safety and comfort of The Queen, the Royal Family and the 300 people who live and work on board are his sole responsibility. Nobody else carries the can. If *Britannia* was to be involved in an incident, it is the Commodore who would have to face The Queen and explain. If the slightest thing goes wrong in any of the complicated moves when the Yacht is being positioned at any one of a hundred foreign ports, the blame falls fairly and squarely on his shoulders.

So, far from being a 'comic opera figure' who is trotted out only for the big occasions, the Commodore is very much a working officer whose experience and expertise is called into daily use by the men under his command. One of the main reasons why *Britannia* functions with 'unobtrusive excellence' – the standard they always aim for – is because the crew are fully aware that the man who leads them has successfully commanded a number of warships and consequently has the experience and confidence to 'drive' the Royal Yacht in any of the conditions she might encounter.

ADEN

IN THE ORIGINAL specification it was stated that *Britannia* could and should be adapted for use as a hospital ship in time of war and in her early days it was certainly feasible for her to have taken on this role.

From time to time various critics voiced their anger that the Royal Yacht had not seen active service when Britain was involved in conflicts where the presence of *Britannia* might have served a useful purpose.

One such occasion was in 1982 during the Falklands Campaign. A number of civilian ships were chartered by the Ministry of Defence to back up the Royal Navy vessels taking part in the fighting. The reason why it was impracticable for *Britannia* to be used was that she required a different kind of fuel from the rest of the fleet and if she had been commandeered it would have meant providing a special tanker to supply her alone. In sheer terms of economy and logistics *Britannia*'s usefulness was far outweighed by the disadvantages. It was a naval decision. The Queen had given permission for *Britannia* to be placed at the disposal of the Admiralty and there is no doubt that it would have been seen as a brilliant public relations coup if the Royal Yacht could have been included. But it didn't happen and the criticism continued.

All this was stilled however, in January 1986, when *Britannia* was involved in one of the most dramatic rescues since the evacuation of Dunkirk in 1940.

The Yacht was sailing from England to Australia and the Pacific Islands in readiness for The Queen's visit when they received a signal from London that civil war had broken out in the former British Protectorate of Aden in South Yemen. A large number of British refugees were waiting on the beach to be taken to safety.

At the moment the signal arrived the Yacht was at the southern end of the

One of the busiest members of the Household is the Travelling Yeoman. He looks after all the luggage of The Queen and the Palace staff. As this amounts to over five tons for every trip, his job is no sinecure. Not only does he make the travel arrangements for the Court and staff, both at home and abroad, he also assists in the Royal servery and makes sure that the correct newspapers and periodicals are distributed to members of the Royal Family and Household wherever they are.

The first of over 1,000 refugees being led from the beach at Aden through the water to the safety of Britannia's waiting boats. (Courtesy of Sir John Garnier)

Red Sea and the annual darts match between the Ward Room and the Petty Officers Mess was taking place. The match was forgotten (for the moment) as *Britannia* immediately set off at full speed for the war zone.

Overnight was busy. The Royal Apartments were cleared in preparation for the accommodation of an unknown number of evacuees, and communications had to be established with the British Embassy in Aden.

Rear-Admiral Sir John Garnier was Flag Officer Royal Yachts at the time. He recalls that the Ministry of Defence also signalled that three other ships, *HMS Newcastle* (Captain P. J. Erskine, Royal Navy), *HMS Jupiter* (Commander R.A.Y. Bridges, Royal Navy), and the Royal Fleet Auxiliary *Brambleleaf* (Captain O. G. Lynch, RFA) had been told to proceed from Mombassa at the

On board the Royal Yacht, warm blankets and hot drinks were waiting as Britannia *sailed from Aden to Djibouti.* (Courtesy of Sir John Garnier)

same time. Subsequently *HMS Hydra* (Commander C. F. Heron-Watson, Royal Navy) sailed from surveying off East Africa, and *MV Diamond Princess* (Captain C. Burtenshaw, Merchant Navy) was loaned by Cunard.

'We were obviously going to get there much earlier, and we in fact arrived off Aden at first light on the morning of 15 January.' (As senior British officer Sir John was in command of the maritime forces allocated to the operation from 15 January until the successful conclusion of the rescue on 24 January.)

Sir John had already spoken to The Queen's Private Secretary, Sir William Heseltine, at Sandringham on the ship-to-shore telephone and he had confirmed that The Queen had instructed that *Britannia* should do all she could to help.

Sir John takes up the story: 'When we got off Aden it was obvious that a lot of fighting was still going on, in fact a full scale battle was in progress with gunboats using the ships in the harbour as shields and firing at the tanks on the shore. I had hoped that we would be able to steam into the Aden Harbour, pick up the British and steam out again.

'This was not to be. Aden Harbour was clearly in the front line of a fairly potent fracas. Also, the British Ambassador, Arthur Marshall, who was doing his utmost to collect all the British residents together, was finding it very difficult to move them with all the shooting going on throughout the area of Aden.

'There were other ships in the area, Russian and French warships, and this posed a special kind of problem because it is illegal to conduct operations in someone else's territorial waters without their permission. Our difficulty was that it wasn't very clear who we could ask this permission from. Our position was also slightly complicated in that the Royal Yacht is a non-combatant ship, but is still a Royal Navy command, so this was a bit of a grey area.

'Protracted negotiations were carried out on 15 and 16 January with a number of different authorities ashore in Aden and, as the situation was very confused, we stayed just outside territorial waters (12 miles) in order not to be the

The Queen gave orders that the State Apartments were to be used during the evacuation from Aden, and the Drawing Room and ante-room were among those turned into temporary dormitories. (Courtesy H.M. Yacht)

cause of any aggravation which might prevent us providing assistance. Eventually we received permission (at 1825 on 17 January) to enter territorial waters and, although this permission was very shortly cancelled, we steamed on in to anchor off Khormaksar beach (at 2005) fully floodlit and with three large White Ensigns at our masts so that there should be no doubt about our identity'.

The scene that greeted *Britannia* was like something out of the Second World War. There were groups on the beaches illuminating themselves with car headlights and bonfires so they could be clearly seen. The boats of *Britannia* were dispatched under the command of the Boatswain of the Yacht (Lieutenant Bob Easson, Royal Navy) as Beachmaster to co-ordinate the evacuation from shore.

Sir John continues: 'We had been told to evacuate the British civilians, but it soon became apparent that we would have to take anybody who was there. In that first night we picked up 152 people of 26 different nationalities, including one French dog. Some of the refugees were in a very distressed condition, having been under fire for some days. All of them were wet to the waist as they had to wade to the boats which could not get closer to the beach as it was too shallow.

'Their reaction when they realised they were being picked up by the Royal Yacht was a sight to see. They couldn't believe it at first. Of all the ships in the world to turn up over the horizon, *Britannia* was the last one they had expected. We tried to make them as comfortable as we could and it turned out that *Britannia* was an excellent choice for the job in hand.

'We had lots of space, good communications, which were important because we had to inform the various countries whose citizens we had on board, and, unlike most modern warships, plenty of small boats to get close inshore.

'We were able to make them reasonably comfortable as we had cleared all the furniture out of the Royal Drawing and Dining Rooms to prepare them as dormitories, and we used all the available cabins to accommodate the women with young children, and some of the injured.

'The next morning we were somewhat surprised to find that all the other ships in the bay had sailed, without saying anything to us, so we were rather on our own. By the time the sun came up at half past six there were many more on the beach than we had expected, and we were not at all sure how many of them we would be able to get on board.

'We started to evacuate the refugees and then at about 8.15 a.m. we had to stop because the boats and the people were coming under fire from sniper bullets. This should have been only a temporary setback as the Beachmaster moved the embarkation point a bit further down the beach out of range of the snipers, and the embarkation was restarted after a delay of only about 15 minutes.

'However, shortly afterwards things started to get a trifle nasty. The oil storage depot at Khormaksar airfield just behind the beach caught fire and then tanks appeared at one end of the beach and began firing at buildings at the opposite end, catching the people in between in the crossfire. The miracle was that nobody was hit, either from the snipers' fire or from the tanks' guns.

'During the morning we evacuated 279 men, women and children, which made a total of 431 on board altogether. We then withdrew outside territorial waters and transferred 81 French nationals to the *Jules Verne* which gave us a bit more room so we went back to the beach where there was very heavy fighting going on by this time. It was quite obvious very soon that, with shells falling in the sea between *Britannia* and the shore, there was little prospect of continuing with the evacuation in the immediate future.

'Therefore, having briefed Captain Erskine (*HMS Newcastle*) and leaving him temporarily in charge in my absence, I decided to sail to Djibouti to disembark those we had onboard, so that we would have more room for further refugees. We arrived at Djibouti just before midnight, and berthed alongside as normal with the floodlights on and with the Royal Marine Band playing suitable music. We disembarked the evacuees with considerable help from the Honorary British Consul (Mr Christopher Reddington) and cleared the Yacht overnight and were ready to sail again at 7.30 the next morning.

'Overnight Captain Erskine had used the sophisticated communications of *HMS Newcastle* to very good effect and, with the assistance of the Embassy Vice Consul (Mr N. Sheppard), had established contact with a number of groups of refugees moving to different points in the Yemen. As a result, we had a much clearer picture of the overall situation and knew that about 200 were moving with difficulty from Wadi Banaa to Zinjibar (about 50 miles north east of Aden), and a further 200 to Mukalla (about 200 miles east of Zinjibar) where the situation was reported as quiet.

'Our first priority was clearly those at Zinjibar. During the day, as *HMS Jupiter* was not permitted to enter territorial waters, Commander Bridges had sent a team ashore from the 12-mile limit in outboard powered dinghies to make contact with the refugees and to mark the embarkation point on the featureless shore. As a result, having passed Aden at 1600 at high speed, we were able to anchor without difficulty off the lights that had been left by *HMS Jupiter*, and *Britannia*'s boats started the embarkation of the refugees at 1900. By 2200, we had collected 209 and moved outside territorial waters to transfer them to *HMS Jupiter*, which took them to Djibouti.

Rear-Admiral (now Sir) John Garnier, Britannia's Commander at Aden, was responsible for saving some 1,068 men, women and children of 55 different nationalities. Here he is seen (left) with the Russian liaison officer during the evacuation. (Courtesy of Sir John Garnier)

Lieutenant Bob Easson, Britannia's *Boatswain received The Queen's Commendation for Bravery for his conduct as Beachmaster during the Aden evacuation.* (Courtesy of Sir John Garnier)

'Over the next 36 hours the negotiations with the shore continued through Captain Saeed Yafai (Aden Port Captain) who, with Mr S. Scadden (Head of Chancery in the Embassy) on board the Royal Yacht, played a particularly important part in representing to the authorities ashore our commitment to evacuate all UK nationals, and our willingness to take anybody else who wished to leave.

'These negotiations led to a series of hopes of further evacuations, which were dashed in turn either by the deteriorating weather or by the fighting ashore which prevented the refugees moving to possible evacuation points. During this time the situation of those stranded ashore was becoming very serious as they were running short of water and food, and it was of course very hot.

'To assist the negotiations, *Britannia* had embarked a Soviet liaison officer from *MV Vinnitsa* in order to improve communication with the Soviet ships and their Embassy in Aden. At the same time strong pressure was being applied by the Foreign and Commonwealth Office through the United Nations. During the morning of 22 January it became clear that these concerted efforts would bear fruit, and we heard that the refugees would be permitted to move from the Soviet Embassy compound where they had been gathered.

'*Britannia* anchored off Little Aden

just before lunchtime, and shortly after we saw convoys moving along the road towards the jetties. By 1700 the evacuation was in full swing to the Royal Yacht, and to Soviet and French ships, and when the shore authorities suspended the operation for the night at 2300 we had embarked a further 227. We started again the next morning and eventually some 441 men, women and children were safely on board.'

As Sir John Garnier gave orders to set sail for Djibouti once more, he received a radio message from shore saying, 'Come back, there's one more waiting here'. So he turned *Britannia* around and went back to pick up the lone survivor on the beach. It turned out he was a London Transport bus driver who had been staying in Aden on holiday with some friends. He had quite a story to tell his family when he got home.

During this same period, 248 more were evacuated from Mukalla by *HMS Newcastle* and *MV Diamond Princess*, and a further 49 from Nishtun by *HMS Hydra*.

Britannia again set off for Djibouti where the evacuees were disembarked overnight on 23/24 January. When the final count was made it was found she had lifted to safety some 1,068 people, out of a total of 1,379 of 55 different nationalities who were rescued by all the naval forces allocated to the operation.

Britannia's original orders had been to rescue British subjects, but as Sir John Garnier said afterwards, 'It would have been inhumane in the very dangerous conditions to have selected on the grounds of nationality, so we took everybody who was able to reach the boats'.

Once the rescue operation was over,

Sir John reported to The Queen that he was resuming his voyage to New Zealand (and the Ward Room and Petty Officers went back to finish their darts match – which the Petty Officers won handsomely). The crew used the time to repair the ravages caused by the unexpected influx of so many guests. By the time they had reached Singapore all traces of the action had disappeared. But the Yachtsmen said that all the refugees, without exception – even those who had no idea they were on the Royal Yacht – treated the ship with respect, and there was nowhere near the amount of damage they might have sustained. Much of *Britannia*'s food stocks had been depleted but that was a minor problem, and the Royal Apartments were soon restored to their pristine condition.

Some months later the Yacht's Boatswain, Lieutenant Bob Easson, received The Queen's Commendation for Bravery for his conduct as Beachmaster. For the Admiral, his officers and Yachtsmen, the incident had come at exactly the right time. For years they had been waiting to prove that *Britannia* was not just another pleasure cruiser, fit to be used only as a rather grand floating hotel.

They had been ready for the call to action and when it came they performed their duties in exemplary fashion. They could be justly proud of the part they, and the Royal Yacht, had played in a dangerous, exciting and thoroughly worthwhile operation. Never again would they be saddled with the tag 'pleasure boat' sailors. When the time came, *Britannia* had seen active service, come under fire, been more than ready, and proved herself very able.

SEA DAYS

THERE IS NOTHING easier than to criticise the Royal Yacht. Even the idea of having such a vessel seems an anachronism these days – and with the annual running costs amounting to some £10 million, trying to justify its retention is a bit like having to defend the indefensible.

It is, without doubt, the most controversial single item of Royal expenditure and has been ever since it was built. Rarely a year has gone by without a Parliamentary question about how much it costs to run, whether it is worthwhile, its cost effectiveness, and demands for it to be scrapped. So the news that the Yacht is to be decommissioned in 1997 was received with cries of self-righteous triumph in some quarters – and total dismay in others.

The costs (which have never been hidden) are well publicised by its critics. But what hasn't been talked about so openly is the fact that every year *Britannia* is used by Government departments free of charge, and on each of these days business worth hundreds of millions of pounds is transacted. Sea Days, which is the title given to these occasions, take place around the coast of Britain, or abroad, to coincide with a visit by *Britannia*. They have proved to

Britannia *moors near London's Tower Bridge, before one of her most successful Sea Days.* (Courtesy H.M. Yacht)

be amazingly successful in promoting Britain's export drive.

One of the Government departments or official agencies such as the Department of Trade and Industry takes over *Britannia* for a day and they invite prominent figures from the world of commerce and industry to attend a seminar on board. The invitations are sent specifically to the chief executives or chairperson of the companies and very few refuse.

When *Britannia* was in California as part of The Queen's State Visit to the west coast of the United States, the President of one of the world's largest aviation companies was asked to a Sea Day. He turned up and said that the reason he had come in person was that although he was not at first enthusiastic about the idea, when his wife saw the invitation she made sure they accepted. As he remarked, 'My wife said there was no way she was not going to come on board the Royal Yacht and see where The Queen lives'. Even the most successful businesspeople find it hard to turn down an opportunity to see for themselves what life is like on board the most exclusive yacht in the world.

When a Sea Day is being planned, the official government agency involved lets

In Miami the local sheriff was determined to have his car pictured with the most famous ship in the world.

Britannia is one of the most glamorous venues in the world, and set against a backdrop of Tower Bridge at night, few can match its spectacular appeal.

the Master of the Household's office at Buckingham Palace know who they would like invited. The maximum number is 120, with about the same number again for the evening reception which follows the day's events.

The Chief Clerk to the Master of the Household, Michael Jephson, then produces the official invitations. These state that: THE MASTER OF THE HOUSE-HOLD HAS RECEIVED HER MAJESTY'S COMMAND TO INVITE . . . to a Sea Day, on board HM YACHT *BRITANNIA*, to be given by (followed by the name of the agency). So the invitation is actually sent in the name of The Queen, which is of course an added attraction.

Occasionally a member of the Royal Family will attend, as on 26 June 1992 when the Scottish Financial Enterprise mounted a Sea Day in the port of Leith, Edinburgh. Then, an extra line was added to the invitation which said: 'Followed by lunch in the Presence of The Princess Royal'.

The people invited are all decision-makers in the companies they represent. At the Edinburgh Sea Day there was the head of a Japanese combine who was considering establishing a plant in Scotland. He had flown from Tokyo at his own expense to hold discussions with executives from the Scottish Financial Enterprise and was only staying in Britain for one night before flying back to Japan. Another guest was the President of one of Italy's most prosperous companies, which had branches in Scotland. He said he wouldn't have missed the chance for the world – and the fact that his wife had also been invited to a reception on board later that same evening really clinched it.

The 120 delegates arrived at the quayside at 9 a.m. They were issued with identity tags. Then the Master of the Household officially welcomed them on behalf of The Queen, while Admiral Woodard did the same thing on behalf of the Yacht. They adjourned to the Dining Room which had been converted into a lecture theatre and the opening address was given by Mr Robin Leigh Pemberton (now Lord Kingsdown), Governor of the Bank of England.

Throughout the morning the delegates were split up into various groups with mutual interests and a number of

At five o'clock in the afternoon, everything on board the Royal Yacht stops for tea, one of the most immutable of all Royal traditions. At sea or ashore, it is always the same: Wafer-thin cucumber and salmon sandwiches, pastries and gateaux, with the tea served in the finest bone china cups, all bearing the Royal Cypher.

business sessions developed. One of the surprising things to emerge – at least to an outsider – was that this was no mere 'talking shop'. Deals were actually being concluded and millions of pounds worth of business was being done.

While the talking was going on in the Dining Room, tables were being laid in the Drawing Room for lunch. The seating arrangements had been carefully worked out in advance and the menu chosen by the Master of the Household, in consultation with the

If a member of the Royal Family takes part in one of the Sea Days it's a great bonus. Here Princess Alexandra chats to delegates before lunch on board Britannia. *(Courtesy H.M. Yacht)*

Everyone lends a hand as the Royal Apartments are made ready for lunch. Seating is completely informal and the business talks continue throughout the meal. (Courtesy H.M. Yacht)

representative of the Scottish Financial Enterprise, who were paying the bills. Another point worthy of mention is that these Sea Days do not cost *Britannia* a penny. All expenses, for food, wine, even coffee and biscuits and the hire of audio/visual aids, are met by the sponsoring agency. All that *Britannia* provides is the premises and the sailors who move the furniture about and wait at table.

When the morning session ends the guests are guided towards the Verandah Deck where pre-lunch drinks are served to the accompaniment of the Royal Marines Band. While this is going on the Keeper and Steward of the Royal Apartments and his team move into the Dining Room and ante-room where they have just 40 minutes to remove all the chairs and other paraphernalia used during the morning, and reconvert the rooms into dining rooms for the remainder of the lunch party. With 120 sitting down it is impossible to get them all into one room so all three State Rooms are used.

It is a very slick operation by now,

with everyone knowing what he has to do. Because it is a team effort there is no demarcation either by rank or trade. The Royal Marines Band help shift heavy furniture, and leading stokers carry flower arrangements which have been prepared overnight.

There is no sign of panic – the Royal Steward describes it as 'controlled chaos'. In fact the only logistics problem he has is with the provision of lavatories. There are none on the decks where the State Rooms are located so everyone has to troop down a flight of stairs to the main deck and use the bathrooms there. It's not a major problem but there can be something of a traffic jam during the 'comfort breaks'.

Meanwhile the Princess Royal has arrived on board. She is meeting and chatting to the guests until the Admiral gets the signal that all is ready down below. He leads Her Royal Highness and the principal guests to the top table and the rest of the party take their places. The most important guests are seated at her table naturally, and she has been given a briefing about them and their companies before she arrived on board.

But apart from the conversation at lunch the Princess takes no part in the day's proceedings. She is there simply to add lustre to the occasion and there is no doubt that having a Royal on board lends an extra air of excitement.

The tables are laid for either six or eight people. They serve themselves from long buffet tables ranged along one side of the room. There are no speeches and lunch takes only about an hour. The Princess Royal leaves and the guests then move back to the Verandah Deck while the rooms are prepared for the afternoon session.

SEE GARAGE FOR ROYAL ROLLS-ROYCE

By mid-afternoon the business of the day is over. The delegates leave for their hotels to get ready for the evening reception which is one of the highlights of every Sea Day.

Spouses are invited to join the delegates. By the time they arrive on the yacht at 6.30 p.m. all traces of the day's seminar have been removed. The State Apartments are back in their original configuration, looking as if nothing has ever been disturbed. The reception is being hosted by the Secretary of State for Scotland, with The Queen's permission. He and Admiral Woodard greet each couple as they arrive.

Britannia's officers are on duty and the stewards serve drinks guaranteed to make the eyes water.

The guests are divided into small parties of half a dozen or so, with one of the officers acting as guide for a tour of the Yacht. They set off at intervals, each one following a prescribed route. They start on the Funnel Deck where they see the Royal Barge and the two 34-ft motor boats. Just below the Funnel Deck is the garage where the Royal Rolls-Royce used to be housed (they haven't actually carried the Rolls since the early 1970s).

Moving across the Flag Deck to the Bridge and into the Wheelhouse they see the wheel which came from the racing yacht *Britannia* which King George V sailed so successfully in the 1920s. Next stop is the Senior Officers Cabin Flat, where there isn't a great deal to see apart from the photographs outside the Admiral's cabin showing all the Flag Officers Royal Yachts since the Second World War: Sir Connolly Abel-Smith, Sir Peter Dawnay, Sir Joseph Henley, Sir Patrick Morgan, Sir Richard Trowbridge, Sir Hugh Janion, Sir Paul Greening, and Sir John Garnier. There are also some unpublished photographs of the younger members of the Royal Family lining the corridor.

The Ward Room is next on the list. It is not very large but includes a comfortable sitting room and bar. Much of the silver came from previous Royal Yachts; most of it is 19th century and the monogram *Victoria & Albert* can clearly be seen on several pieces. There is a silver sailing ship standing behind the bar which is the top half of a salt cellar. This was presented to the officers of the *Victoria & Albert III* at Cowes in 1909.

Another prized possession is the silver gilt punch bowl which was presented to the Yacht by the Czarina of Russia in 1909. The lamp fittings came from the

---

There is a refrigerated store on board in which fresh flowers are kept. Often these have been brought from the Royal Gardens at Windsor, but the Steward who arranges them in the Royal Apartments also buys local flowers in the countries visited.

Victoria & Albert III, while the figure of a monkey arrived in the Ward Room in 1957 after a Royal visit to Copenhagen. He is moved daily and is said to get quite cross if neglected.

Just behind the Commander's place at the dining table is a photograph of The Queen and the Royal Family in an informal pose during the Western Isles cruise.

The visitors' route then takes them into the Yacht's laundry and down into the engine room which is so clean that a number of visitors have asked if this is just for show, with another 'working' engine room elsewhere. But this is the only one, complete with the original 42-year-old engines and a 'golden rivet' on the port side, which your guide informs you is there 'for the benefit of those who

do not believe in it!'

In the Royal Servery visitors marvel at the compact neatness of the ovens, hot plates and storage cupboards. Then comes the moment they have all been waiting for, an opportunity to see inside the Royal Apartments.

The Dining Room looks as it does when The Queen is on board, with the magnificent mahogany table laid for dinner, floral displays all around, and the gold centrepieces sparkling. Visitors then move into the ante-room, and from there to the Drawing Room which has had all its furniture reinstated. The grand piano, Queen Victoria's satin-wood writing desk, Prince Albert's gimbal table, all the things they have heard and read about are there for them to see. And finally up the Grand Staircase into

Following the evening reception, to which delegates' spouses are also invited, guests line the decks to watch the highlight of the day – Beat Retreat. This is at Leith in Scotland.
(Photograph by David Hunt)

the Sun Lounge before going back onto the Verandah Deck for another drink.

The evening is not over yet. There is still one more experience to come. This is the ceremony of Beat Retreat when the Band of the Royal Marines forms up on the quayside and marches and counter marches in a dazzling 25-minute display of precision drills, playing familiar and favourite tunes. The guests line the rail. It is the perfect end to a perfect day as the band marches off and reluctantly we take our leave, being formally saluted by the Yacht's Commander as we do so.

The people from the Scottish Financial Enterprise add up the benefits

The Queen takes a personal interest in all the soft furnishings in the Royal Apartments. She chooses them herself, spending hours sorting through samples and pattern books. Nothing is ever thrown away.

of the Sea Day and they are delighted. Millions of pounds worth of business has been transacted, Scotland has been brought to the forefront of international trade, and *Britannia* has once again shown that when it comes to staging a conference, hosting a party, and adding that little something extra, no one can beat her.

WHAT NEXT?

H.M.Y. BRITANNIA

AS SHE ENTERED the fifth and final decade of her service, *Britannia* was now the oldest ship in the Royal Navy which still went to sea. Nelson's flagship, *HMS Victory*, though permanently laid up in Portsmouth, was still technically in commission.

In the 43 years of her life the Royal Yacht had seen many changes. The political map of the world had altered beyond recognition, with some of the countries she visited in her early days disappearing completely.

Kings, Queens, Presidents and Prime Ministers had all been entertained on board with equal hospitality whether they had come from republics, friendly monarchies or totalitarian regimes. The welcome had always been the same for each of them; the State Banquet organised with exactly the same ceremony for the most powerful nations on earth or the tiniest principalities.

Men had been knighted on *Britannia*'s decks, and marriage banns had been read thousands of miles from the church where the wedding was to take place.

Business deals worth hundreds of millions of dollars were concluded over the State dining table, and every member of the Royal Family had come to regard the ship with affection.

There was one other distinction which made *Britannia* unusual. In the present day Royal Navy, she was one of the few ships which regularly fulfilled its original design function and had done so since the day she was commissioned.

The grey warships are designed primarily to fight: aircraft carriers, frigates, destroyers and mine sweepers all exist either to be used in time of war, or as a deterrent.

In the past 44 years, since *Britannia* was launched, some – not every one by any means – have been involved in fighting in various parts of the world, most recently in the Adriatic and the Gulf, and before that in the Falklands Campaign of 1982. Going back even further, Royal Navy ships saw action in Korea in the 1950s, the Malayan Emergency and

As in all Royal residences The Queen and Prince Philip had separate bedrooms. When the Yacht was being fitted out, great care was taken to ensure that each of them was given exactly what they wanted. For example, they both prefer blankets and sheets to duvets, but the dimensions of Her Majesty's bedclothes differ from those of His Royal Highness. This is because Her Majesty likes a deeper turnback.

The Duke of Edinburgh sitting at Queen Victoria's desk in the Drawing Room on board Britannia. (Photographers International)

Indonesian Confrontation, and in the Icelandic 'Cod Wars'.

It is a proud record, but nevertheless a large proportion of warships in the Royal Navy are commissioned, used for training, refitted, worked and then paid-off some 20 or 25 years later, never having fired a shot in anger. This is not to say they haven't earned their keep; their very presence has been necessary to ensure peace in various parts of the world and they have performed their tasks admirably.

The Royal Yacht was built as a floating home for The Queen and her family. That was the original intention, and from the day she was commissioned, 11 January 1954, she had been used every

Her Majesty appearing to have some trouble with her tiara as she leaves Britannia *for dinner ashore during the 1994 D-Day ceremonies.* (Terry Fincher)

year for State Visits, official banquets and receptions, Royal honeymoons and the annual summer cruise. She saw action in Aden in 1986, and the public and private sectors used her facilities frequently for their business seminars.

In other words the Royal Yacht regularly fulfilled its design function; it did what it was always intended to do.

With her original cost of just over £2 million and her annual running costs nearly five times that amount, the yacht had long been a sitting target for critics of Royal expenditure. Her various refits had pushed the amount spent on her to well over £100 million; in 1987-88 alone it rose to £22.4 million, and again in 1991–92, to £12.5 million (see Appendix). In the final two years of her sea-going life an increase in *Britannia*'s use for Sea Days did much to offset her

running costs. In 1992/3 there were six, each of which generated business in excess of £200 million. These were contracts that were actually signed, not just vague promises made in the euphoria of the moment.

The Foreign Office and the Department of Trade and Industry were convinced that by using *Britannia* in this way they were able to attract enormous benefits to British industry. Working on the basis that very few people would turn down an invitation to spend a day on the most famous ship in the world, it gave them a platform on which to build contacts at the highest level. And the personal involvement of members of the Royal Family from time to time was an added bonus which few business executives, British or foreign, could resist.

One of Britannia's *many ports of call during her 43 year life. This is Helsinki.*

In terms of cost effectiveness *Britannia* came out surprisingly well. In 1991 an exercise was carried out using a proposed State Visit to Japan as the blue-print. The Queen and the Duke of Edinburgh would have travelled with an entourage of 45, which meant that an entire hotel would have had to be taken over. The hosts were apprehensive of the security risks if the Royal party shared their accommodation with other guests. It would also have been necessary for all food and drink to be taken from Britain for the duration of the visit. Other venues would have had to be hired in order that The Queen could hold official dinners and receptions for her hosts.

CHEAPER TO USE SHIP THAN HOTEL

During the five days of the State Visit the local police and security forces would have been stretched almost beyond their capacity providing round-the-clock cover at the hotel and in the surrounding buildings. Finally, the cost of transforming part of the hotel into suitable accommodation for the Royal party, and establishing the necessary communications network, escalated the overall budget of the trip to several million pounds.

Using *Britannia* as a base meant that the ship had to position herself in Japan, a round trip of some three months. This was obviously the biggest single item of expense and there was no way it could be avoided. However, once in Japan the Yacht could be used for all the Royal party. Everyone knew exactly where they were supposed to be, and the provisions for all meals and functions were to be brought from home as usual.

The Queen would have been able to offer reciprocal hospitality to her hosts on board *Britannia*, security was much

Grace was not said before dinner — or any other meal — and even though The Queen and her guest of honour exchanged toasts, speeches were kept to a minimum. Smoking was not encouraged at the table, but Her Majesty had no objection to guests doing so in the Drawing Room either before or after dinner.

easier and cheaper to provide, and as a final clincher, a Sea Day was planned which would have made huge profits for those attending.

When the two methods were compared, it emerged that it would have been cheaper to use *Britannia* for the State Visit. And by using the Royal Yacht, The Queen would have been able to show the flag in the most practical fashion, demonstrating the British way of doing things and leaving no-one in any doubt about the identity of the country she was representing.

Of course, it is too easy to build the case you want on figures alone. Any competent statistician can make anything he wishes out of practically any combination of numbers, and there was no disguising the fact that *Britannia* was an expensive luxury. But it also provided a practical solution to a number of problems that arose whenever The Queen had to visit a foreign country. Those listed were the most serious in terms of sheer logistics. But one enormous benefit that could not be quantified in monetary terms was that when Her Majesty returned to *Britannia* after a long day's work, which might involve several different engagements, she did feel that she was coming back to her own home.

All the rooms, the furniture, the decorations were familiar, as indeed they should have been because she chose them

Nowhere was the Royal Yacht more welcome than when she was carrying The Queen and her family on the Western Isles summer cruise.

all. If she wanted to, Her Majesty could throw off her shoes, put her feet up and relax, exactly as she could at any of the Royal homes. What was to stop her doing that in an hotel, or at the British Embassy or High Commission of the country she was visiting? Nothing really, except that

nobody feels at home in an hotel, no matter how luxurious. If she did stay at a Government residence, the strain on the local man and his resources would be intolerable, as has been proved on numerous occasions when this has been unavoidable. The Queen recognises this.

Britannia was without doubt the most cossetted ship in the world. Every nut, bolt and rivet was inspected regularly and her engines, though 43 years old, still managed to propel her for a range of 2,500 miles at a speed of 14 knots, with a maximum speed of 21 knots. The Yacht had now completed more than one million miles on those original engines.

In 1992 it was decided to inspect the hull to see if the years had taken their toll on the steel plates. It would have been reasonable to expect some of them to be showing signs of wear and tear, but when she was brought out of the water it was discovered that the only part of the vessel where the steel was getting a bit thin was near the bows where the constant chaffing of the anchor chain had caused some weakness. Apart from this minor defect *Britannia* was as good as new. She was in truly spectacular condition for a lady of her age.

To build another *Britannia* to the same specifications as the present Royal Yacht would cost in excess of £200 million at today's prices. This is clearly a non-starter. Neither The Queen nor the Government would countenance spending such a sum.

Obviously no government is going to advocate such expenditure on what they recognise would be a very unpopular item, without solid arguments to the contrary. Politically it would be highly dangerous in the first instance. The Prime Minister who authorised the spending of such a large amount of money would need to feel very sure of himself and confident of his ability to persuade the country that he was acting in the best interests of all concerned, not just the Sovereign.

But if we pause for a moment to consider all the implications – and the alternatives – it might well turn out that an order for a new Royal Yacht could be just the shot in the arm that

Queen Elizabeth The Queen Mother followed by the Princess of Wales during the ceremonies to mark the 50th anniversary of D-Day. (Terry Fincher)

The Duke of Edinburgh, wearing the uniform of Admiral of the Fleet, with the Princess of Wales at the D-Day anniversary. This was the last picture taken of Diana, Princess of Wales, on board Britannia. (Terry Fincher)

the British economy needs.

In the first place the contract would obviously have to be placed with a British shipyard. The idea of a foreign company building the Sovereign's personal yacht would be unthinkable. British shipbuilders are the best in the world and this would be their chance to show what they can still do. It would be the showpiece vessel of the 21st century, combining the latest technical innovations with the very best that modern designers can produce, to provide a truly majestic yacht for The Queen and her successors, at a realistic price.

The new Royal Yacht would not need to be anywhere near as large as *Britannia*, and the furniture from the present yacht could be adapted to fit the dimensions of the new vessel. So there would be no great additional expense involved in fitting her out.

In addition, if the yacht were to be designed from the start as a floating business centre, using all that is best from the Royal Apartments, and combining the latest technology – audio/visual aids, satellite communications, laser printers, and all the other paraphernalia the modern business executive demands – its use could be divided between the Royal Family and industry on an equitable basis, making the project self supporting.

The Palace encouraged the practice of Sea Days involving *Britannia*. How much more palatable the idea of a replacement would be if right from the start everybody knew precisely how much it was all going to cost, and that the money was going to come from industry and commerce who would be using the yacht on a regular, fee paying basis. We could end up with a Royal Yacht that actually made a profit and did not cost the taxpayer a penny!

The alternative would probably mean chartering commercial aircraft and prohibitively costly hotel accommodation at least twice a year for the State Visits. The huge security problems would have

If any of the younger children in the Royal Family were on board they would eat separately from the adults, but with almost as much preparation and under strict supervision, so that by the time they were ready to join the senior members of the family at meals, they were fully aware of the protocol involved and how to behave properly. Royal training begins at a very early age.

to be met by the host countries at considerable expense and inconvenience, and the ultimate result might be a reduction in overseas travel by The Queen: some countries could be reluctant to assume the extra responsibilities and costs.

Also the status of the Sovereign and the country would be affected if there

A Royal farewell. The Queen and the Duke of Edinburgh wave from the Verandah Deck as an escort launch hovers nearby. (Jayne Fincher)

The crowd's farewell. Their enthusiasm says it all.

was no Royal Yacht to carry the flag to the four corners of the earth.

If we accept the need for a continuing role for the Monarchy in Britain it is important that we do not allow any devaluation in that role.

Wherever Monarchy is spoken of – anywhere in the world – the words 'The Queen' refer to only one person – Elizabeth II. Her position as the world's leading Monarch is unassailable and will remain so as long as the dignity and status of her lifestyle stays at the highest level.

The Royal Yacht was an integral part of that lifestyle, and also of the working routine of the Monarchy. *Britannia* has proved to be a brilliant success story in the past 43 years; surely, in a nation with as proud a maritime history as Britain's it is not to be the last Royal Yacht?

THE FINAL VOYAGE

ON MONDAY 20 October 1997 *Britannia* slipped her moorings and sailed out of her home port of Portsmouth on the first leg of her final voyage as a Royal Yacht.

After 43 years in commissioned service, she was setting off around the coastline of Britain, calling in at her last eight ports before returning to Portsmouth to be paid-off.

Thousands of men, women and children lined the shore and waved a fond farewell as she headed for Devonport, the first of her ports of call, where a warm welcome awaited her.

After that, *Britannia* sailed up the coast of Cornwall and North Devon and into the Bristol Channel towards Cardiff, where Prince Edward hosted a dinner and several receptions on board.

Then it was across the Irish Sea to Belfast, where similar functions were planned, before heading back into English waters, to spend two days in

The Queen and the Duke of Edinburgh pose with the full Yacht's company during the last Western Isles cruise in August 1997. (Courtesy H.M. Yacht)

Her Majesty, accompanied by Britannia's *last Commander, Commodore Anthony Morrow, on her final visit to the Yacht in Portsmouth.* (PA News)

Liverpool. There was a tremendous feeling of nostalgia as she sailed into Glasgow, for it was on Clydeside that she had been built, at the John Brown & Co shipyard, and it was here that The Queen had launched her in 1953. Leaving Glasgow the Yacht sailed due north to Aberdeen, one of the cities which had seen her more frequently than any other, apart from Portsmouth.

It was at Aberdeen that Her Majesty always disembarked following her annual Western Isles cruise at the start of her summer holiday at Balmoral (Her Majesty made her last voyage in the Yacht in August 1997).

The granite city had always had a particular affection for *Britannia* – and the Yacht's complement regarded Aberdeen as their Scottish home from home.

A poignant moment as The Queen and the Duke of Edinburgh step ashore from Britannia *for the last time after she has completed 43 years of unblemished service.* (PA News)

The Paying-Off Ceremony in Portsmouth on 11 December 1997 is attended by fourteen members of the Royal Family, including The Queen's four children. (Tim Graham, Sygma)

From Aberdeen, they sailed south to Newcastle, before leaving for London where she berthed in the shadow of Tower Bridge, surely one of the most familiar sights in the world. Such was the interest in the capital, and so many people wanted to see her, that *Britannia* stayed in London for a week with a formal lunch, dinner and reception being held every day. The Duke of Edinburgh, who had taken such a personal and active part in the Yacht's design, acted as host to a dinner party which raised several thousand pounds for King George's Fund for Sailors, one of the Royal Family's favourite charities.

Britannia arrived back in Portsmouth on 22 November after just over a month away, to prepare for her final Royal duty, the decommissioning and Paying-Off Ceremony.

Prince Edward, followed by Sophie Rhys-Jones, Peter Phillips and the Duke of York, walks down the gangway for the last time as Captain Tim Laurence, the Princess Royal and the Prince of Wales wait to disembark. (Tim Graham, Sygma)

As a fitting gesture, The Queen had ordered one of her family to be on board at each of the towns and cities on this last emotional voyage. The Prince of Wales, the Duke of York, Prince Edward, the Princess Royal, the Duke of Gloucester, the Duke of Kent and Princess Alexandra, all represented Her Majesty as *Britannia* made her stately progress around Britain. It truly was a case of A Royal in every port.

THE PAYING-OFF

Her Majesty's Yacht *Britannia* paid-off on Thursday 11 December 1997 at the Portsmouth Naval Base in the presence of The Queen, the Duke of Edinburgh and 12 other senior members of the Royal Family. It was a dramatic, emotional and moving occasion as they were joined by 2,200 past and present Royal Yacht Officers and Royal Yachtsmen,

who had been specially invited to witness the final act of Royal maritime pageantry. And The Queen had requested that their families should also be included in the day's events, so there was a wonderful mixture of the formal and informal as young children ran about enjoying the occasion while their parents sat dressed in their finery quietly exchanging memories of days gone by – and now, sadly, never to return.

Although the Government had said that *Britannia* was to be 'decommissioned' the term 'paying-off' was used by the Royal Navy to describe her last day. The reason was that previous Royal Yachts had traditionally been paid-off into reserve or disposal. The future of *Britannia* was uncertain at the time of the paying-off as the Secretary of State for Defence, Mr George Robertson, had not made a final decision on where she would spend the rest of her days. At the

Some 2,200 guests, mainly past and present members of Britannia's *crew and their families were invited to witness the Royal Yacht's paying-off.* (Tim Graham, Sygma)

time of writing, he had indicated that the choice was between Manchester and the port of Leith in Edinburgh. This news was received with great dismay in Portsmouth, her home port – and indeed, where Royal Yachts have been based since the 18th century – which many people felt was her natural berth. Many of the Yachtsmen, who were retiring from the Royal Navy when they left *Britannia*, had hoped to continue their association with the Yacht in a civilian capacity.

The debate about *Britannia*'s fate attracted wide attention, both at home and throughout the world, wherever seamen gathered. Some felt she should be preserved at all costs and moored alongside her famous sister, *HMS Nelson*, in permanent drydock in Portsmouth. As a venue for tourists she would have been an obvious attraction. One of the problems though was that few people realized just how small were the areas visitors would be able to see. The Royal Apartments consist of only

three rooms basically: the Drawing Room, Ante Room and State Dining Room, hardly enough to compete with the romantic attractions of Nelson's flagship. It might have been possible to keep The Queen's and Prince Philip's sitting rooms as they were, but even these are so small that it would be impracticable to allow more than six or seven people in at a time.

The Royal bedroom cabins, once they had been stripped of their Royal artifacts, look exactly like any other cabin, so they would hardly be considered worth paying to see. And while there would certainly be an initial interest in visiting the Royal Yacht, it is doubtful if she could be maintained as a commercial enterprise without large sums of money being spent on her upkeep. Paying visitors would, quite rightly, expect the Yacht to look as it did when The Queen and her family were on board, in the same way that Buckingham Palace and Windsor Castle are obviously 'living' Royal residences.

The Royal Yacht makes stately progress up the River Thames during her farewell tour of the United Kingdom in 1997. (PA News)

The floodlit Britannia *at Tower Bridge, flying her paying-off pennant.* (PA News)

Another suggestion was that *Britannia* should become a floating education centre, located in one of the country's less favourable areas so that young people might have an opportunity of using this historic ship as a focal point in their studies. Again there were practical reasons why this, seemingly excellent and worthwhile, idea could not be adopted. *Britannia* has been used many times for business seminars and conferences, but only on a temporary basis which has involved a considerable amount of work being carried out on a voluntary footing by large numbers of Yachtsmen and members of the Royal Household. And one major obstacle is the shortage of lavatories and bathrooms on board. It was always a serious logistical problem when organising functions on *Britannia* to make sure that sufficient facilities were available.

HMY Britannia *beneath one of London's most historic landmarks, Tower Bridge, during her final farewell tour.* (Courtesy H.M. Yacht)

There was also a number of frivolous suggestions, including using her as a floating casino or hiring her out to firms who might want to entertain their wealthiest clients on the most prestigious yacht in the world.

It was the ever practical Princess Royal who put into words the thoughts of many of those who had been involved with *Britannia*, when she suggested that perhaps it might be a fitting end to this gallant old vessel to simply take her out to sea and scuttle her. And this was not as outrageous as it sounds, even if it was one of the most politically incorrect statements of 1997, causing Her Royal Highness to be attacked in the media as someone who was 'totally out of touch with the ordinary people'. The Princess pointed out that *Britannia* needed her large crew to maintain her in the pristine condition we had come to expect. Without those dedicated Yachtsmen to polish her brasses and keep her super-

structure as new, she would soon become a sad sight. (Anyone who saw the Royal Yacht in the weeks following her decommissioning, as she lay in her berth awaiting the Defence Secretary's final decision, would agree that she was indeed a sorry sight – a pale reflection of her original splendour.) Who is to say that the Princess Royal was wrong when all she was advocating was to allow *Britannia* to end her days with dignity?

All this was still very much in the air while *Britannia*'s final and most historic role was being played out. Although there are no hard and fast rules about the ceremonial procedures for paying-off, it is traditional that a pennant, a long flag bearing the Cross of St George, is flown from the mainmast immediately prior to paying-off.

The pennant is usually the length of the vessel (412-ft for *Britannia*) plus one foot for every year that the vessel has

HMY Britannia *makes her triumphant final entry into her home port of Portsmouth accompanied by a flotilla of small craft.* (Courtesy H.M. Yacht)

Flying her paying-off pennant of over 400 feet representing one foot for every year she was in commission plus the length of the Yacht.
(Courtesy H.M. Yacht)

been in commission. *Britannia* flew her paying-off pennant on leaving London on 21 November and again on her return to Portsmouth the following day. She also flew it on the final Sunday that she was in commission, 7 December.

Before the Paying-Off Ceremony began The Queen, accompanied by the rest of the Royal party, embarked for a final private visit to the Yacht, where they said a personal farewell to the Officers and Yachtsmen during a last tour of *Britannia*. Among the guests were previous Flag Officers Royal Yachts and their wives, and in a much appreciated gesture Her Majesty had also invited the widows of former Flag Officers. A particularly welcome figure was Rear-Admiral Sir Robert Woodard KCVO, the last Admiral to command *Britannia*, who was knighted by The Queen in the romantic setting of his own quarter-deck on the final day of his naval career, during the State Visit to South Africa in 1995. The First Sea

Lord, Admiral Sir Jock Slater (himself a former Royal Yacht Officer) and the Secretary of State for Defence, Mr George Robertson completed the party as Commodore Anthony Morrow hosted a buffet lunch on board before the formalities began.

With the Paying-Off Ceremony due to begin at 3 o'clock, the Yacht's Company performed the complicated manoeuvre required to 'Man Ship.' Whenever The Queen has embarked in the Royal Yacht at the beginning of a period of Royal duty and when she disembarks at the conclusion, the Royal Yacht Officers and Yachtsmen have traditionally manned ship. On this solemn occasion they were carrying out the duty for the last time. The Yacht's company took up their places on the upper decks at a measured, slow march, moving into view from aft until they filled the entire upper decks. The drill was all the more impressive as it was carried out – as always – in silence. There were no spoken words of command. All timings and drill placings were controlled by the Yacht's Executive Officer, Commander Simon Martin, with the use of a buzzer that was inaudible to the watching crowds.

The entire operation took just ten minutes and then the Royal party came ashore with The Queen being the last to leave *Britannia*. As Her Majesty stepped on to the gangway she was piped ashore. Normally she is the only person to be piped on and off *Britannia* although, as a mark of personal favour, she had ordered certain foreign Heads of State to be piped on board on a few occasions. It was a compliment that was greatly appreciated.

The custom of 'piping' goes back many centuries, with a Bosun's whistle, sometimes called a pipe or call, being used to warn the ship's company of the arrival of a distinguished guest. The pipe has been a badge of office for a Commanding Officer in the Royal Navy since the reign of Henry VIII (1509–1547).

On *Britannia*, the Bosun was in charge of the full Piping Party of six Royal Yachtsmen and the Coxswain. The Bosun himself used a gold pipe which dated from 1805 and was presented to The Queen by the Royal Navy Club in 1954.

Once the Royal Party had been seated in the Royal Box, the Service of Thanksgiving began. It was conducted by the three most senior naval clergy, representing all Christian denominations: The Chaplain of the Fleet, The Principal Chaplain of the Church of Scotland and Free Churches, and the Principal Roman Catholic Chaplain. The service was drawn up to reflect the

A picture that needs no explanation! (Courtesy H.M. Yacht)

Able Seaman Jay Sowerby mans the wheel as Britannia *leaves Portsmouth for her final five-week farewell tour of the United Kingdom.* (PA News)

HMY Britannia *alongside in Hong Kong in July 1997, acting as a Royal residence for the Prince of Wales during the handing-over of the colony to China.* (Courtesy H.M. Yacht)

usual Sunday services held on board *Britannia* at sea. It was simple, devout without being too pious, and very emotive. No-one present could have failed to be moved by the sadness of the occasion – or the dignity with which The Queen and her guests said goodbye to a much-loved Royal home. Following the religious service, the Band of the Royal Marines performed the ceremony of Beat Retreat, marching and counter-marching in front of *Britannia* playing some of Her Majesty's favourite tunes. Royal feet were seen to be tapping in time with the music until the focal point of the parade – the lowering of the flags – was reached.

As the band played *Sunset*, the Union Flag at the jackstaff, the Lord High Admiral's Flag at the foremast, the Union Flag at the mizzenmast and the White Ensign at the stern, were all dramatically lowered for the last time. It was the moment when the watching crowds finally realized that *Britannia* was decommissioned. It was a silent and solemn occasion for all those present – and for the millions watching this live on television as it was beamed around the world.

The Royal Marines played *Rule Britannia*, then the National Anthem, and marched off to the strains of *Hearts of Oak*, the march past of the Royal Navy, and the last tune heard was The Regimental March of the HM Royal Marines, *A Life on the Ocean Wave.*

Suddenly it was all over. As the guests dispersed to join the Royal Family for tea in adjacent buildings which had been specially decorated for the occasion, one of the yacht's former officers, Lt Cdr Bob Henry, who was for ten years Keeper and Steward of the Royal Apartments, summed up the feelings of everyone. 'It's a sad day for The Queen, it's a sad day for the Royal Navy, and it's a sad day for the country.' What else was there to say?

After more than 300 years of continuous service, Britain no longer has a Royal Yacht.

FACTS & FIGURES

For the statistically minded, *Britannia* was actually in commission as a seagoing Royal Yacht for 43 years and 334 days. During that period, she steamed a total of 1,087,623 nautical miles and carried out 968 visits overseas and in home waters.

The Queen and other members of the Royal Family were carried for 696 official visits abroad and 272 Royal visits around the British Isles.

In the last 12 months of her life, the Yacht hosted 67 major commercial and diplomatic events, earning millions of dollars in export orders for British industry.

Her longest voyage, lasting eight months, began in January 1997 and ended in August, during which she visited 17 countries and carried out 28 visits.

Leaving Portsmouth, she headed for Malta, Egypt and the Yemen, before calling at the United Arab Emirates, Pakistan, India, Thailand, Malaysia, Japan and South Korea. This epic voyage provided an opportunity for ambassadors and diplomats to renew relationships, make new friendships on behalf of Britain and forge a lasting harmony between the United Kingdom and many foreign countries.

A total of 83 trade and business appointments were concluded on board the Yacht, with many of the world's leading companies taking advantage of

Hong Kong's last British Governor, Chris Patten, boards the Royal Yacht on his final day, carrying the Union Flag from Government House. (Courtesy H.M. Yacht)

Dressed overall,
The Royal Yacht
Britannia *is*
moored in her home
port of Portsmouth
before being
decommissioned on
11 December 1997.
It was the last time
she would fly the
Royal Standard.
(PA News)

this unique opportunity. The focal point of this historic voyage was Hong Kong, where she was to act as an official Royal residence to the Prince of Wales for the duration of his stay in the colony prior to its handing back to China.

Hong Kong was a magnificent setting for *Britannia*, and Prince Charles, representing The Queen, offered hospitality to a variety of individuals and organisations who had gathered to witness the historic events of July 1997.

It somehow seemed appropriate that torrential rain should pour down on that final evening as the handing-over ceremonies took place. The Royal Marines Band played and fireworks exploded as Britain's last Governor of Hong Kong, Mr Chris Patten, and his family, joined the Prince of Wales on board as *Britannia* sailed away from the former colony for the last time. As in so many of the voyages in her long and distinguished career, the Royal Yacht had a significant role as once again history was being made. She proved to be an important player on the international stage as this last chapter of the British Empire was finally closed.

On her return voyage to Britain, the Royal Yacht called at Manila, Crete and Gibraltar, and everywhere she went she was used to promote the interests of the British people.

In April 1998, it was announced that *Britannia* would be given a permanent final berth in Leith, Edinburgh.

THE FUTURE

The Defence Secretary's decision to hand *Britannia* over to the City of Edinburgh, where she will spend the rest of her life, came after a brilliant campaign which not only stressed the emotional ties between the former Royal Yacht and Scotland, but also included a most comprehensive business plan.

It was not enough simply to try to persuade the Government that *Britannia* should end her days in the same part of the world where she had been built as the politicians and civil servants demanded hard evidence that the people who were bidding for her, knew what they were doing and, more importantly, that they had done their sums – and had got them right.

Reassurances were needed that

The Queen's Bedroom on the Shelter Deck complete with the original furnishings. This is the first time a bedroom of a living sovereign has ever been on public display. (Eric Thorburn)

Prince Philip's Bedroom is identical in size to the Queen's, but reflects his personal choice of fittings with single bed and plain covers. (Eric Thorburn)

Britannia's dignity and prestige would continue to be maintained at the highest level. Forth Ports, the successful bidders, had worked for months in preparing their bid. They knew how much they could afford to pay for the yacht and exactly how much more they would need to restore her to her former pristine condition. A concerted effort was made by bringing people with sound commercial experience together with planners, designers, tourist authorities and the developers of Leith Dockside, where *Britannia* was to find her future, permanent berth. The campaign was mounted with military precision, with every possible query anticipated – and it paid off.

The final price paid for *Britannia* was £250,000 – her scrap value. It could be said that this has to be the nautical bargain of the decade. In terms of sheer publicity value alone, just being able to use the name, *Britannia*, is said to be worth millions.

What Forth Ports got for their money was a ship that had been virtually stripped of everything associated with the Royal Family but what they ended up with was a yacht fully equipped with practically every original item of furniture, all the paintings, personal photographs, priceless carpets, the Royal grand piano, and even the crystal, silverware and dinner services used by Royalty when they were on board. So the *Britannia* that the paying visitors see today is in almost every respect exactly as it was when The Queen and her family sailed in her.

The first thing the new owners had to

do was to get the yacht from Portsmouth, where she had been decommissioned, around the east coast of Britain to Edinburgh, so that they could start work on her. This was no easy task as *Britannia* was no longer able to sail under her own steam; her engines had been decommissioned also, so it was necessary to engage the services of an ocean-going tug to tow her. It was not the most auspicious moment in the proud life of the former Royal Yacht, particularly when no British vessel could be found to perform the task. Instead, a German-owned tug was chartered and so we had the sorry spectacle of the most famous ship in the Royal Navy being towed out of her home port of Portsmouth for the last time, by a foreign tug.

Britannia was welcomed back to Edinburgh by vast, enthusiastic crowds who had gathered to see her enter the historic dockside at Leith.

But they only had a brief opportunity of viewing her as she was immediately sent into dry-dock for the massive face-lift she so desperately needed. Only six months after her decommissioning, the ship's appearance had deteriorated drastically. She was surveyed from top to bottom, bow to stern, and then work was begun straight away to return her to the immaculate condition she had enjoyed for over 40 years. Not only was it necessary to restore the State Apartments, but also the other working parts of the yacht as these too were going to be open to the public. Both the Royal Navy side, containing the

By far the largest cabin on the yacht is the Commodore's day cabin where he used to entertain guests and hold meetings with his senior officers. (Eric Thorburn)

The State Dining Room is now used for special corporate events where even the menus reflect Britannia's *glorious career.* (Eric Thorburn)

Commodore's day cabin, various mess-decks, the engine room, and the Royal quarters, were to be included in the tour. In addition, *Britannia* had to be equipped to make access possible for disabled people.

Structurally the yacht was in first class condition, but to minimise the risk of unnecessary corrosion the propellers were removed as was anything else that might be inclined to rot. She was completely repainted and then moved to Edinburgh Dock where the work on her interior was carried out. New electrical and ventilation systems were installed, extra joinery work was necessary and security systems and fire alarms had to be fitted.

Once this work had been completed, the task of replacing the Royal furniture and artefacts was started. Using photographs taken when the Royal Family were on board, and with help from the yacht's former crew, the rooms were painstakingly reconstructed.

There were lengthy negotiations involving senior officials of the Royal Collection, who had to be satisfied that there was going to be a dignified presentation reflecting the previous regal image of *Britannia*. Once they were convinced, 95 per cent of the original furniture was returned to the yacht on permanent loan. There is even a display of Royal cutlery in the Silver Pantry.

The State Drawing Room and Ante Room are in exactly the same condition as when the Royal Family were on board, with precisely the same chairs, sofas, tables and carpets. And now, for the first time, the Royal bedrooms can be seen by the public, with the Queen's and the Duke of Edinburgh's cabins viewed through glass panels installed in the walls. It was an ingenious way of solving the problem of how to allow people to see the bedrooms without cutting a further doorway to permit through traffic. Visitors are also experiencing a slice of Royal history as never before has the bedroom of a living monarch been shown, either on land or at sea.

The restoration is so accurate that one might be forgiven for expecting to see the Royal couple appear at any moment!

Many of the gifts given to the Queen during her State Visits abroad are displayed, reflecting the yacht's million miles of global travel to the four corners of the Earth.

The onshore Britannia Visitors Centre was designed by Sir Terence Conran, and before boarding the yacht, visitors can see an exhibition which tells the complete story of *Britannia*. A state of the art technical area includes CD-ROM and touchscreen facilities. There is the 41ft Royal Barge floating in its own pool, the gleaming wheelhouse and the ornately carved antique binnacle which came from the old Royal Yacht, *Victoria & Albert*, and which later stood on the Shelter Deck of *Britannia*. Sections of the crew's quarters have been removed from the yacht and installed in the visitor centre to show the contrast between the naval

The Ward Room. All the original furniture has been obtained so that today it looks exactly as it did when the yacht was at sea. (Eric Thorburn)

Britannia's *priceless collection of silver cutlery is displayed in the Silver Pantry. Some of these items date back to the reign of King George II.* (Joe Little)

Britannia *being towed into Leith Docks in April 1998, where she was welcomed to her final berth after 43 years at sea.* (Courtesy *The Scotsman*)

side and the Royal accommodation.

Throughout there are many photographs from the unique *Britannia* archives, illustrating brilliantly how various members of the Royal Family have enjoyed their time on board since she was commissioned in 1954. Visitors are loaned a handset which gives them an audio guide in one of five languages as they move around *Britannia* independently as there are no formal tours. Everyone is left to look around at their leisure with approximately 50 people allowed on board every 20 minutes or so. On an average day some 1,500 visitors view the yacht.

As well as being open throughout the year, *Britannia* is now also used for corporate entertaining. Suitable companies are able to hire the yacht for an evening and guests are treated as Royalty. They board *Britannia* via the Royal Brow, a privilege previously reserved for members of the Royal Family and other Heads of State, this being a welcome on board by *Britannia*'s own Pipe Major. A reception is held in the State Drawing Room with dinner served in the State Dining Room, followed by escorted tours around the Royal Apartments.

Britannia opened its doors to visitors for the first time in October 1998 and up to 200,000 people a year are expected to experience this unique opportunity. Today the former Royal Yacht is owned by a charitable trust with all profits being ploughed back for its upkeep and to pay the salaries and expenses of the permanent staff.

Britannia will never go to sea again;

Work continued night and day as the former Royal Yacht was restored to her original superb condition in readiness for the hundreds of thousands of visitors waiting to come aboard. (Courtesy *The Scotsman*)

Sir Terence Conran designed the magnificent Britannia Visitors Centre, which houses a spectacular exhibition telling the story of this historic ship. (Courtesy *The Scotsman*)

she has dropped anchor for the last time. Her days as the pride of the fleet are over but she remains a national treasure and as such she must be protected and cherished. She deserves no less. In Edinburgh the ship has been restored to much of her former glory to serve as a constant reminder of Britain's immortal maritime heritage and she now has a secure future after a dignified and magnificent past. *Britannia* is still truly, a Palace afloat.

STATE, OVERSEAS AND UK OFFICIAL VISITS, 1954–1997

1954	Libya	The Queen, The Duke of Edinburgh, Prince Charles and Princess Anne
	Canada	The Duke of Edinburgh
1955	West Indies	Princess Margaret
	Mediterranean	The Duke of Edinburgh
	Norway	The Queen and The Duke of Edinburgh
	Wales, Isle of Man, and Scotland	The Queen, The Duke of Edinburgh, Prince Charles and Princess Anne
	Denmark	The Duke of Edinburgh
1956	Mediterranean	The Queen and The Duke of Edinburgh
	Sweden	The Queen and The Duke of Edinburgh
	Scotland	The Duke of Edinburgh
	Kenya, Mauritius, Zanzibar and Tanganyika	Princess Margaret
1956–1957	World Tour	The Duke of Edinburgh
1957	Portugal	The Queen and The Duke of Edinburgh
	Denmark	The Queen and The Duke of Edinburgh
	Channel Islands and England	The Queen, The Duke of Edinburgh and Prince Charles

1958	Netherlands	The Queen
	Northern Ireland	Queen Elizabeth, The Queen Mother
	Great Britain	The Queen and The Duke of Edinburgh
1959	Pacific Islands, Panama and the Bahamas	The Duke of Edinburgh
	Canada	The Queen and The Duke of Edinburgh
1960	Caribbean Islands	Princess Anne
	West Indies	Princess Margaret and Mr Antony Armstrong-Jones honeymoon
1961	Gibraltar and Tunisia	Queen Elizabeth, The Queen Mother
	Italy	The Queen and The Duke of Edinburgh
	Greece and Turkey	The Duke and Duchess of Gloucester
	England and Northern Ireland	The Queen and The Duke of Edinburgh
	Ghana, Liberia, Sierra Leone, The Gambia and Senegal	The Queen and The Duke of Edinburgh
1962	Gibraltar, Cyprus and Libya	Princess Anne

	England	Queen Elizabeth, The Queen Mother, The Queen and The Duke of Edinburgh	1970	Fiji, Tonga, New Zealand and Australia	The Queen and The Duke of Edinburgh
1963	Fiji, New Zealand and Australia	The Queen and The Duke of Edinburgh	1971	Panama Canal & Pacific Islands	The Duke of Edinburgh
	Channel Islands	Queen Elizabeth, The Queen Mother		Canada	The Queen, The Duke of Edinburgh and Princess Anne
	Isle of Man and England	Queen Elizabeth, The Queen Mother		Turkey	The Queen, The Duke of Edinburgh and Princess Anne
1964	West Indies	Queen Elizabeth, The Queen Mother	1972	South East Asia	The Queen, The Duke of Edinburgh and Princess Anne
	Scotland	The Queen and The Duke of Edinburgh		Channel Isles	Princess Anne
	Iceland	The Duke of Edinburgh	1973	West Indies and The Galapagos Islands	Princess Anne and Captain Mark Phillips honeymoon
	Canada	Princess Anne visited Newfoundland. The Queen and The Duke of Edinburgh visited Charlottetown and Quebec	1974	New Zealand, The Far East and Australia	The Queen and The Duke of Edinburgh
	The Bahamas and West Indies	The Duke of Edinburgh	1975	Mexico	The Queen and The Duke of Edinburgh
				Central America	The Duke of Edinburgh
1965	Netherlands	Princess Margaret and Lord Snowdon		Jamaica	The Queen and The Duke of Edinburgh
	West Germany	The Queen and The Duke of Edinburgh		Channel Islands	Queen Elizabeth, The Queen Mother
	Britain	The Queen and The Duke of Edinburgh	1976	Finland	The Queen and The Duke of Edinburgh
1966	The West Indies	The Queen and The Duke of Edinburgh		USA and Canada	The Queen and The Duke of Edinburgh
	Australia, Fiji and New Zealand	Queen Elizabeth, The Queen Mother	1977	Samoa, Tonga, Fiji, New Zealand and Australia	The Queen and The Duke of Edinburgh
1967	Canada	The Queen and The Duke of Edinburgh		United Kingdom	The Queen and The Duke of Edinburgh
1968	Brazil and Chile	The Queen and The Duke of Edinburgh		West Indies	The Queen and The Duke of Edinburgh
1969	Wales	The Queen and The Duke of Edinburgh for the Investiture of The Prince of Wales	1978	West Germany	The Queen and The Duke of Edinburgh

	Channel Isles	The Queen and The Duke of Edinburgh
1979	Eastern Arabia	The Queen and The Duke of Edinburgh
	Denmark	The Queen and The Duke of Edinburgh
	Great Britain	Queen Elizabeth, The Queen Mother
1980	France	The Prince of Wales
	United Kingdom	The Queen and The Duke of Edinburgh, Queen Elizabeth, The Queen Mother
	Italy	The Queen and The Duke of Edinburgh
	North Africa	The Queen and The Duke of Edinburgh
1981	Norway	The Queen and The Duke of Edinburgh
	Shetland	The Queen and The Duke of Edinburgh
	Mediterranean and Red Sea	The Prince and Princess of Wales honeymoon
	Indian Ocean and Australasia	The Queen and The Duke of Edinburgh
1982	England	Queen Elizabeth, The Queen Mother
	Australia and The Pacific Islands	The Queen and The Duke of Edinburgh
1983	Mexico, USA and Canada	The Queen and The Duke of Edinburgh
	Sweden	The Queen and The Duke of Edinburgh
	Canada	The Prince and Princess of Wales
1984	France	The Queen and The Duke of Edinburgh
	Canada	The Queen and The Duke of Edinburgh
	Italy	Queen Elizabeth, The Queen Mother

1985	Portugal	The Queen and The Duke of Edinburgh
	Niger, Mali, Gambia, Senegal, Madeira and Mauritania	The Queen and The Duke of Edinburgh
	Italy	The Prince and Princess of Wales
	Belize, Bahamas, St Kitts-Nevis, Antigua, Dominica, St Lucia, St Vincent and The Grenadines, Grenada, Trinidad and Tobago	The Queen and The Duke of Edinburgh
1986	Azores	The Duke and Duchess of York honeymoon
	China and Hong Kong	The Queen and The Duke of Edinburgh
	Oman, Qatar, Bahrain, Saudi Arabia	The Prince and Princess of Wales
	Cyprus	The Prince of Wales
	Australia	The Queen and The Duke of Edinburgh
1988	Barbados, Costa Rica, The Galapagos	The Duke of Edinburgh
1989	Spain	The Queen and The Duke of Edinburgh
	Channel Islands	The Queen and The Duke of Edinburgh
	Singapore and Malaysia	The Queen and The Duke of Edinburgh
	Java, Indonesia, Malaysia and Brunei	The Duke of Edinburgh
	Hong Kong	The Prince and Princess of Wales

1990	Iceland	The Queen and The Duke of Edinburgh
	Nigeria and Cameroon	The Prince and Princess of Wales
1991	USA	The Queen and The Duke of Edinburgh
	Brazil	The Prince and Princess of Wales
	Wales	The Duke of York
	Canada	The Prince and Princess of Wales
	Belem (Brazil)	Business Leaders Forum led by Minister for Overseas Development
1992	Malta	The Queen and The Duke of Edinburgh
	France	The Queen and The Duke of Edinburgh
1993	Dominica, Montserrat, Nevis, St Kitts, Anguilla, British Virgin Islands, Turks & Caicos Islands	The Duke of Edinburgh

	East Coast of England	The Queen and The Duke of Edinburgh
	Mexico	The Prince of Wales
	Cyprus	The Queen and The Duke of Edinburgh
	Turkey	The Prince of Wales (Sea Day)
	Saudi Arabia, Abu Dhabi	The Prince of Wales
	Palm Beach	Scotch Whisky Industry
	London	London Forum & London First
	Abu Dhabi	British Gas
	Bombay	Indo-British Initiative
1994	The Caribbean and Latin America	The Queen and The Duke of Edinburgh
	UK/France	Members of the Royal Family (D-Day Commemorations)
	London	The Prince of Wales
1995	South Africa	The Queen and The Duke of Edinburgh
1996	Russia	The Queen and The Duke of Edinburgh
1997	Hong Kong	The Prince of Wales

SEA DAYS

1968	Brazil	To promote trade.
1975	Mexico	To promote trade.
1976	New York	British Trade Development Board in USA.
1980	Naples	British Invisibles.
1983	Stockholm	British Invisibles.
1985	Lisbon	DTI British Technology Seminar.
1986	Adelaide	British Invisibles.
	Shanghai	DTI.
1988	Los Angeles	British Invisibles.
	Barcelona	British Invisibles.
1989	London	British Invisibles.
	Malaysia	British Invisibles.
1990	Brazil	British Invisibles.
1991	Miami	DTI.
	Tampa	DTI.
	Lisbon	Scottish Financial Enterprise (BI).

	London	British Invisibles.
1992	Rome	British Invisibles.
	Stockholm	British Invisibles.
	Leith	Scottish Financial Enterprise (BI).
1993	Istanbul	British Invisibles.
	Athens	British Invisibles.
	Bombay	British Invisibles.
1994	New York	British Invisibles.
	Helsinki	British Invisibles.
1995	Capetown	British Invisibles.
	Terna	British Invisibles.
	Dakar	British Invisibles.
	Piraeus	British Invisibles.
	Lisbon	British Invisibles.
1996	Boston	Welsh Development Agency.
	Toronto	British Invisibles/Locate in Scotland.

	Belfast	Irish Development Board.
	Amsterdam	British Invisibles.
1997	Aden	DTI.
	Dubai	British Invisibles.
	Karachi	DTI.
	Mumbai	DTI.
	Chennai	DTI.

Singapore	DTI.
Bangkok	British Invisibles.
Tokyo	British Invisibles.
Nagoya	DTI.
Kobe	DTI.
Inchon	British Invisibles.
Gibraltar	British Invisibles.

OTHER RELATED BUSINESS EVENTS

1990	London	General Council of British Shipping.

	London	British Invisibles.
1992	Leith	EC Summit Dinner.

The end of the rainbow? A dramatic view of Britannia *moored on the River Thames, 21 November 1997, overlooked by the centuries-old Tower of London, one of the Capital's most historic and famous landmarks. (G. Rickwood)*

Technical Description

H.M.Y. BRITANNIA

ACCOMMODATION

Accommodation for the Royal party and staff is aft, and for the ship's company forward.

The Royal apartments are on the shelter deck between the main and mizzen masts with a verandah at the after end leading on to a sun deck. A point which may be noticed from the profile is that the deck of these apartments is 2-ft higher than the general shelter deck level so that the external fore and aft gangways are well below the windows of the Royal apartments.

The main staircase from the Royal apartments on the shelter deck leads to a vestibule on the upper deck about which are grouped the State apartments. At either side of the vestibule are Her Majesty's and His Royal Highness' sitting rooms. The dining room, drawing room and ante-room extend the full width of the superstructure without obstruction from pillars. Sliding screens are fitted at the entrance to the ante-room and between the ante-room and the drawing room. They can be folded back when required to provide a large reception space from the after end of the drawing room to the foot of the main staircase.

The main staircase down from the upper deck to the main deck, in the vicinity of the main entrance ports. The Household and guest cabins, sitting rooms and cloakrooms are on this deck. These rooms are fitted out to first class passenger liner standards.

The Royal staff is accommodated on the lower deck, the rooms being fitted out to Service standards.

A passenger lift is fitted near to the main staircase and operates between the main and shelter decks.

The crew of 21 officers and 256 men is accommodated forward in a manner generally in accordance with Service practice except that the CPOs occupy 4-berth cabins.

LAYOUT AS HOSPITAL SHIP

In the initial stages of the design the Medical Director General of the Navy was consulted about the requirements for the vessel in her role as a hospital ship. It was thus possible to proceed with the designs for a hospital ship and a Royal Yacht concurrently, so that the conversion could be made in the most economical manner. In consequence, relatively little alteration to existing structure and equipment would have been required in the event of war making conversion necessary.

The wards to accommodate 200 patients were located in the after part of the ship. Most of the patients would be medical and surgical cases requiring normal hospital conditions, but provision was also necessary for zymotic (infectious) cases and those suffering from tuberculosis. Zymotics would be accommodated in glazed cubicles built within the drawing room, and these cubicles, together with toilet and sanitary facilities, would be isolated from the remainder of the hospital. Tuberculosis cases requiring 'fresh air' beds would be accommodated on part of the verandah, whilst others suffering from this disease would be berthed in wards in the space now occupied by the Royal bedrooms. The remaining wards, including the cabins and ward room for sick officers, and cabins for a few female patients, would be sited in the other Royal apartments and in spaces now allocated to members of the Royal Household and staff.

Particular care was taken in the layout of bathrooms and sanitary facilities to ensure that as little alteration as possible would be necessary upon conversion.

The operating theatre, with its annexes and adjacent steriliser and anaesthetic rooms, was on the lower deck. There were also other specialist facilities there including an ophthalmic room, a physiotherapy room, a pathology laboratory and an X-ray room with dark room. Full facilities for dental treatment including a laboratory were to be located on the main deck.

For the care and treatment of the patients, the naval medical complement would comprise eight medical and dental officers, five nursing sisters and 47 male ratings.

GALLEYS, COLD AND COOL ROOMS

Separate galleys are provided for the Royal party, the ship's officers and the ship's company, all grouped amidships on the upper deck. The exhaust ventilation trunks from these spaces are led up inside the funnel.

Ranges, grills and ovens are all electric, steam being supplied only for steam cookers and boiling coppers. The usual ancillary equipment is installed.

The Royal galley provides service for the Royal dining room and also for the Royal staff messes, the food for the latter being conveyed by lift to the lower deck. This galley is of such a size and is so equipped that for hospital ship service it could provide suitable food for all the patients.

Lifts from the crew's galley take food direct to the main and lower decks for distribution to the various crew messes. The enclosed messes on the main deck are provided with pantries fitted with hot cupboards and automatic refrigerators. Food for the lower deck broadside messes is distributed from a large servery on the lower deck, this servery also being equipped with adequate hot cupboard and automatic refrigerator capacity.

Four main cold and cool rooms are provided for the storage of provisions. The two cold rooms (10°F) for meat and fish, one for the Royal party and the other for the ship's company, are large enough to provide supplies for 45 days for the ship's company, and considerably longer for the Royal party. The dairy room (32°F) and the fruit and vegetable room (35°F) are of sufficient capacity to meet the total requirements of the ship for 30 days.

An ice making cabinet in the cooling machinery compartment makes 500 lb of ice per day, and incorporates storage capacity for 1,000 lb.

The cooling machinery for the cold and cool rooms for ice-making consists of two electrically-driven water-cooled, cooling plants using Freon 12/Arcton 6 as the refrigerant, each machine being fitted with independent control valves.

The cold and cool rooms, as in modern naval practice, are refrigerated by air re-circulation. Normal brine arrangements are provided for the ice-tank.

AIR-CONDITIONING, VENTILATION AND HEATING

An air-conditioning system serves the after accommodation spaces which in the hospital ship role will be the hospital section of the ship. This system has been designed to maintain an inside condition of 85°F dry bulb and 71°F wet bulb when the outside atmospheric condition is 88°F dry bulb and 80°F wet bulb. Under cold weather conditions the installation will maintain an inside temperature of 70°F when the outside temperature is 30°F.

The refrigerating machinery for air-conditioning comprises two steam jet vacuum type plants each capable of extracting 1,000,000 BTUs per hour under tropical conditions. The cooling medium is chilled water circulated to 13 air-conditioning units, each of which serves a particular section of the ship. The heating medium is warm water circulated to the units through heating calorifiers. Automatic temperature and humidity controllers are provided for each section.

Special attention has been paid to the ventilation installation, and care has been taken to keep noise levels to a minimum. Fans and units have been grouped in acoustically lined chambers and where necessary trunking has also been acoustically lined. The low speed commercial type fans which have been adopted assist in reducing air noises and the fans themselves are on resilient mounts.

No re-circulation of conditioned air is used in the system, fresh filtered air being supplied whether cooling, heating or mechanical ventilation is in operation.

The forward accommodation spaces for the ship's company are ventilated by fan supply and exhaust; they are heated by Admiralty pattern gilled tube type heaters in the fan supply capable of maintaining an inside temperature of 70°F when the outside temperature is 30°F. These systems are manually controlled, only temperature being regulated by means of bypass valves in the heater units. Galleys, bathrooms, workshops, etc., are ventilated with air at atmospheric temperature by fan supply and exhaust.

A separate small refrigerating unit is fitted to air-condition the wireless offices.

Every effort has been made to ensure that the ventilation system is fitted with the least possible detriment to the water-tight integrity of the ship. All ventilation trunking is arranged so that no main sub-division bulkhead is pierced below deck. To preserve the watertightness of the plat-form deck the ventilation trunking from hold compartments is watertight between the platform and lower decks except when the trunking leads to a fan on the platform deck. In such cases a watertight slide valve is fitted to the trunking at platform deck level.

Above the main deck the fire division bulkheads are fitted with valves each side, where pierced by ventilation trunking. Watertight slide valves are also fitted to trunking piercing the foremost and after-most subdivision bulkheads.

The large inlets to supply fan spaces in the sides of the upper deck superstructure are provided with portable covers which can be fitted in an emergency.

PUMPING, WATER AND OIL SERVICES

FIRE AND SALVAGE SYSTEM

Britannia has a large pumping capacity which fully meets the Ministry of Transport requirement for pumping and fire-fighting.

Three 70-ton/hour motor driven bilge pumps are fitted, one in each of the three main machinery spaces, also one 70-ton pump is fitted aft of the machinery spaces and one 20-ton pump forward. The 70-ton pump in the boiler room is an emergency submersible pump with controls geared to above the main deck. Each pump can take suction from the sea, from the compartment in which it is situated, or from the main suction line. Discharge is overboard or to the fire main. The main suction line runs throughout the ship, being well above the keel outside the machinery spaces. Suctions are provided in all the principal compartments below the platform deck.

The fire main runs throughout the length of the ship with adequate hose connections for fire-fighting within the ship and on the weather decks. Foam arrangements are provided for fire-fighting in the machinery spaces. An automatic sprinkler system is fitted throughout the after accommodation. This system is powered by a separate sprinkler pump and can be cross-connected to the fire main should the sprinkler pump break down.

Sanitary services are supplied from the fire main through reducing valves. As a safeguard against loss of pressure in the fire main, a separate sanitary pump is fitted in the system aft.

FRESH WATER SYSTEMS

Allowance has been made for a higher rate of consumption of fresh water for domestic purposes than is usual in HM ships. Tank stowage for 195 tons of fresh water is provided although it is usual for only 120 tons to be carried, and there are two evaporators with a total distilling capacity of 120 tons per 20-hour day. A 20-ton/day feed-water distilling plant is fitted in the engine room to provide make-up feed water.

Fresh water storage tanks are fitted at each end of the ship. Two separate fresh water pressure supply systems are provided, one forward and one aft, and can be inter-connected if required. Two 10-ton/hour pumps supply the after system and one 10-ton pump the forward system. The water is chemically treated by the injection of chlorine into the filling main. The water is pumped from the storage tanks through fine mesh filters to the pressure tanks and then to the fresh water main through carbon dechlorinators. A small quantity of lime is added to the water in the storage tanks to make it slightly alkaline and so protect the copper piping of the systems.

Separate hot fresh water systems are also fitted forward and aft with provision for inter-connecting. Each system is heated by a 300 gallon steam calorifier with a heating capacity of 3,000 gallons per hour. A 1-hp circulating pump is fitted in each system.

FUEL OIL SYSTEM

Capacity is provided for 490 tons of fuel oil and 20 tons of diesel oil. The tanks are situated mainly in the double bottom, although deep tanks are located fore and aft of the machinery spaces. Settling tanks are provided, port and starboard, in the boiler room.

Filling connections are fitted amidships and forward, and fuel may be embarked either side of the ship. The forward position is used mainly for replenishment at sea, for which a standard naval light jackstay rig is provided. It is expected to achieve a fuelling rate of 250 tons/hour at sea.

An oil fuel suction main runs the full length of the oil fuel tanks with branches to each tank. The oil fuel filling line is connected to this suction main in the boiler room and the tanks are filled through the suctions. To prevent undue pressure coming on to the filling line a relief valve is fitted with discharge to the settling tanks. Oil can be transferred from the forward to the after tanks and vice versa, should it be required to transfer oil to correct heel or for any other purpose. It cannot, however, be transferred from the port to starboard tanks in the same group.

SEWAGE SYSTEM

Careful consideration was given during the design to the arrangements for disposal of sewage and waste water. The problem was important because of the probability that the ship, in either role, could be required to lie in restricted, perhaps non-tidal, harbours for long periods with her full complement on board.

Two entirely separate sewage and waste water systems are fitted, one forward and one aft. This will enable the system aft to be completely shut down when it is not required. Each system discharges to a sewage tank which is pumped out by either of two pumps operated by float control. Two overboard discharges are provided, one each side of the ship for each system and either pump may discharge either side. The sewage tank may be bypassed if necessary.

The size of the sewage tanks which could be fitted was limited by the space available. In order to reduce the frequency of pumping out the tanks when necessary, arrangements were made for the disposal of waste water from baths directly overboard in harbour.

EQUIPMENT

ANCHORS AND CABLES

The anchor and cable equipment consists of:

- 3 60-cwt Admiralty pattern stockless bower anchors (one spare)
- 270 fathoms of $1^7/8$ in. forged steel stud link cable
- 1 20-cwt Admiralty pattern stockless cast head type steam anchor
- 1 300-lb Danforth kedge anchor

Recessed stowages are provided for the bower anchors, port and starboard, and considerable care was taken to get a good working arrangement consistent with keeping the size of the anchor recesses to a minimum. A 1 in. scale model and later a full scale mock-up were produced to ensure the development of satisfactory hawse pipes and recessed stowages.

A twin-headed electrically driven capstan and cable gear is fitted forward driven by a 6.4 hp motor slung beneath the fo'c'sle deck. The cable holders are suitable for working $1^7/8$ in. steel cables and the barrels are suitable for $4^3/4$ in. wires. The capstan is capable of exerting a pull on either cable, but not simultaneously of 20 tons at 25 ft./min. and hoisting slack cable equivalent to a pull of $1^1/2$ tons at 40 ft./min. The gear is capable of exerting a pull greater than 48 tons but the clutches are designed to slip at a load of 50 tons. A warping pull of 15 tons at 33 ft./min. is possible from either capstan barrel and the brake gear is capable of holding 30 tons without creeping.

No arrangements are fitted for catting the anchors; special fairleads are fitted at the bow port and starboard for use when securing to a buoy or when being towed.

An electrically-driven capstan is fitted aft for working $4^3/4$ in. steel wire hawsers; it can exert a pull of 5 tons at 25 ft./min and heave in slack at 40 ft./min.

BOATS AND LIFE-SAVING EQUIPMENT

The boat complement is large by Service standards for the size of ship, and consists of:

- 1 40-ft Royal barge
- 2 35-ft medium speed motor boats
- 1 32-ft motor cutter
- 2 27-ft jolly boats (sea boats)

2 16-ft fast motor dinghies

2 14-ft sailing dinghies

The 35-ft motor boats are of round bilge form, and not designed to achieve planing speed. The acceptance of medium speed permits the installation of robust diesel engines. The main consideration governing the hull construction has been lightness in association with maximum strength.

In the 27-ft jolly boats the engine has a closed circulation system which enables it to be started up with the boat in the davits, so ensuring that the engine is running properly before the boat is water-borne.

All power boats are diesel driven.

In addition to the life-saving capacity of the boats, *Britannia* carries 18 life rafts. They are of a self-inflating type, stowed on board in valises and weigh with stores about 440 lb each. The raft consists of an oval-shaped float with centre thwart and floor and an arched canopy, all of which are inflated by CO_2 under pressure. Each raft comfortably holds 20 persons. The raft in its valise is thrown overboard secured to the ship by static line. If the line is pulled the raft inflates. Trials have shown that the rafts inflate the right way up irrespective of how they enter the water.

The six larger power boats are stowed in overhead type gravity davits. Single part falls are provided for the rapid lowering of the sea boats, the other boats using two part falls. The 40-ft and 35-ft boat davits are fitted for power hoisting and lowering and emergency gravity lowering, and the 32-ft and 27-ft boat davits for power hoisting and gravity lowering.

A special reeling device has been designed by the davit manufacturers to ensure that the falls lower easily under no load conditions without the need for over-hauling. This device consists essentially of driving the wire mechanically over the pulleys at each davit head. For appearance the davits can be hoisted in-board when the boats are away and by this reeling device the falls can be lowered quickly when the boats have to be hoisted. The 16-ft and 14-ft boats are stowed on the shelter deck amidships and are lowered from the gravity davits using spreaders, after the other boats are away.

DERRICKS AND HOISTING GEAR

Two large derricks are provided amidships, heeling one each side at the base of the funnel. To preserve appearances, derrick posts or cranes were considered undesirable, and a scheme has been devised whereby the funnel has been used as a derrick post. Topping lifts are taken to eye plates which hinge back inside the funnel when not in use; portable cover plates preserve the outward funnel shape. The additional time taken to rig these derricks has been accepted for the sake of appearance.

Power lifting and topping is provided by two winches, each with a working load of two tons. The derricks may be used for storing ship, or as an alternative method of lifting out the motor and sailing dinghies, or for the removal of boat engines from boats in their davits. Spare motor boat engines are carried on board in a motor boat engine workshop so that if necessary engines may be changed at sea with the boats in the davits.

At the after end of the fo'c'sle portable storing davits are fitted, port and starboard, having a working load of 7-cwt, power provided, if required, from the capstan.

A space for a motor car is provided on the shelter deck abreast the 40-ft barge. The car is carried on a transporter running on an athwart-ship trackway sunk into the wood deck and terminating under the 40-ft barge davits. The transporter and car are hoisted outboard on these davits after being raised to the davit head by wires from an hydraulic ram incorporated in the transporter.

STABILISERS

Denny-Brown single fin stabilisers are fitted in a hold apartment immediately forward of the main machinery spaces. The specification for the gear called for power to stabilise a roll of 20 deg. out to out reducing it to 6 deg. out to out at ship speed of 17 knots. The fins, which are retractable, are 4-ft 6-in wide, with outreach from the hull of 9-ft 4-in and area of 42-sq ft each. They are capable of operating at the full ship speed of 22 knots at the maximum fin angle which is 20 deg.

The fins are run out, rotated and retracted by an electro-hydraulic system capable of being controlled from the bridge. The main controlling motor is a $37^{1}/_{2}$ bhp unit and the servo-motor a 10 bhp unit.

NAVIGATION AND COMMUNICATIONS

For navigational purposes the vessel is equipped with an Admiralty (Sperry type) gyro compass installation. The master gyro is situated on the platform deck under the bridge with repeaters to the Royal chart house, compass platform, wheelhouse, bridge wings, steering compartment and emergency conning position.

An ornamental binnacle, originally from the *Royal George*, has been taken from the *Victoria & Albert*, fitted with a gyro repeater and mounted on the sun deck aft.

Magnetic compasses and associated equipment to Admiralty standards are fitted on the compass platform, in the wheelhouse and at the emergency conning position.

The wheel from the racing yacht *Britannia* is used in the wheelhouse and has been suitably inscribed.

In addition, the following navigational aids are installed:

(a) M/F Direction Finder for general use
(b) Decca Navigator
(c) Loran
(d) Navigational Radar Type 974
(e) Commercial type electric log
(f) Echo sounder

RADIO EQUIPMENT

Four transmitting sets and their associated receivers are provided for MF-HF transmission and reception. One set is provided with its own battery equipment for emergency use if all the other power supplies, including the emergency generator, fail. The transmitters are designed to transmit in key or speech. A link is provided for ship-to-shore telephone communication, and on certain phones speech can be scrambled for security purposes if required.

With the number of sets to be operated, whip aerials have to be used in addition to roof aerials. The whips are situated on the bridge and on the sides of the funnel.

The decorative caps on the tops of the masts are aerials.

For the conduct of State business on board, cryptographic equipment is fitted in the cypher office.

Facsimile transmission is also installed.

Sound reproduction equipment is fitted throughout the ship with the choice of three programmes.

SALUTING GUNS

It is a traditional practice to fire a morning and evening gun when Her Majesty is on board her Yacht with her Standard flying, and for this purpose two 3-pdr saluting guns are carried on the compass platform. This practice is no longer in use.

MAIN AND AUXILIARY MACHINERY

The main machinery in *Britannia* consists of two sets of turbines and gearing, each set comprising one HP turbine and one LP turbine in which is incorporated the astern turbine, all constructed by Messrs John Brown & Co (Clydebank) Ltd. Single reduction hobbed and shaved gearing is fitted, driving the shafts at 285 rpm when the maximum power of 6,000 shp per shaft is being developed. Full power revolutions of the HP and LP turbines are 4,910 and 3,550 rpm respectively. The condensers, which are of the two-flow type, are under-slung beneath the LP turbines and are supplied with circulating water by electrically driven pumps with a maximum capacity of 10,000 gall./min. for each condenser. A conventional close-feed system is fitted using an auxiliary condenser in the boiler room for harbour steaming conditions.

Steam is generated from two main boilers, each having a capacity of 75,000-lb./hr. at a pressure of 300-lb./in.^{2} and a temperature at the superheater outlet of 660°F.

The boiler combustion air is trunked to the boilers. It is drawn by electrically driven forced draught fans from a plenum space at the base of the funnel into which the exhaust ventilation from the boiler room is discharged. Thus, warm ventilation exhaust from the boiler room is fed to the boilers augmented by fresh air from the atmosphere drawn through slats in the plenum space.

The exhaust gases from the boilers are extracted by electrically driven induced draught fans and discharged through grit arresters to the atmosphere. At full power the gases leave the funnel with a velocity of about 110-ft./sec. and a temperature of 400 deg.

It is essential for the efficient operation of the grit arresters and to keep the funnel discharge well clear of the ship, that a high efflux velocity of the exhaust gases be maintained under varying power conditions. This is obtained by hydraulic control from the boiler room platform of the inlet flaps to the grit arresters, which allows the number of arresters in use to be adjusted to suit the power.

An auxiliary boiler is installed to meet harbour requirements. It has an evaporating capacity of 20,000 lb./hr. at the same steam conditions as the main boilers, and can be used to augment the main steam supply.

The main and auxiliary boiler feed pumps and the main engine auxiliaries are electrically driven. Two salt water evaporating and distilling plants, each having an output of 60 tons per day, are fitted in the generator room and a 20 tons per day feed water evaporator is sited in the engine room for make-up feed purposes.

The boiler room is supplied by two axial flow fans of 10,000 cu. ft./min. each, while the generator room has a fan supply and exhaust of 15,000 cu. ft./min.

STEERING GEAR

The steering gear is of the electro-hydraulic type with two separate motor-driven variable delivery pumps either of which is capable of actuating the rudder under maximum torque conditions. The pumps are telemotor controlled from the wheelhouse and by mechanical control in the steering gear compartment. A separate hand-operated variable delivery pump is available for emergency operation of the gear. The steering gear is capable of exerting a maximum torque of 200 ft. tons.

FUNNEL

The size and shape of the funnel were finally decided with the assistance of the Aerodynamics Division, NPL, who conducted wind tunnel tests of various funnel designs for the Admiralty.

It was desired that the funnel should have a pleasing appearance, that the decks should be free from smoke and funnel gases, and that the funnel paintwork should not be discoloured by smoke and gases eddying in the vicinity of the funnel top.

A gutterway is fitted around the top of the funnel so that rain water can be drained away to prevent discoloration of the funnel sides. Exhausts from the galley, laundry and lavatory fans, and from the diesel generator and incinerator are led up inside the funnel.

ELECTRICAL INSTALLATION

The following generators are fitted in *Britannia* for lighting and power supplies:

    3 500 kW steam turbo-generators
    1 270 kW diesel generator
    1 60 kW emergency diesel generator

The d.c. installation in *Britannia* is at constant voltage of 225, all permanent wiring being on the two wire, two conductor system with both poles insulated.

The three turbo-generators are fitted in the generator room and any two are capable of supplying the full sea-going load. The 270 kW diesel, also fitted in the generator room, is capable of meeting the harbour load or the salvage load when steam is not available. To allow for maintenance of this diesel generator in harbour when necessary, steam can be supplied from the auxiliary boiler to run one of the turbo-generators to cover the harbour load. The generators feed into a main switchboard in the generator room. Distribution from the main switchboard to the various circuits is by double pole circuit breaker, switches and fuses following normal practice.

The emergency diesel generator, together with its own starting battery, is situated in a shelter deck compartment to meet MOT requirements. It feeds into a switchboard fitted next to the generator and in an emergency will supply vital services such as radio, salvage pumps, emergency lighting and the power operated water-tight doors. An emergency battery is fitted to come into operation for a maximum period of half an hour on failure of the main supply, and to carry the load of essential emergency circuits until the emergency generator can be brought into operation.

A.c. services are supplied by two d.c./a.c. motor generators of output 35 kVA, 23 volts, 50 cycle, single phase. An a.c. switchboard is fitted with two control panels to distribute the power required for radio, sound reproduction equipment, X-ray, cinema and echo sounding.

Two 220/24 volt a.c./d.c. motor generators with control gear, a 24-volt secondary battery, and a switchboard are fitted in the low-power room for supplying the gyro compass equipment, log, telephones, gongs, alarm bells etc.

A permanent system of degaussing is fitted and is fed from the 225 volt system.

Fluorescent lighting has been fitted in messes, offices, workshops, galleys and bathrooms.

The lighting in the Royal and State apartments is generally by wall bracket and ceiling fittings, although in the dining room some concealed fluorescent lighting has been used.

Arrangements are made for flood-lighting the ship and for the customary outline illumination.

Britannia was the first service ship to be fitted with electric battery feed emergency navigational lanterns instead of oil burning emergency lights.

SEA TRIALS

A full programme of contractor's sea trials

– which included speed, turning, manoeuvring, and consumption – was successfully completed in November 1953.

During the measured mile speed trials on the Arran course, a full speed of 22.85 knots was obtained with the ship at 4,320 tons displacement and the machinery developing 12,400 shp at 289 rpm. The propulsive coefficient related to the naked hull ehp deduced from the model results at full speed was 0.6. There was a moderate sea and wind speeds at times reached 50 knots. The wind was more or less on the beam and caused the ship to heel to leeward a few degrees; during a particularly heavy gust it reached 10 deg. Rudder angle of about 4 deg. was necessary to maintain a steady course in the most adverse conditions.

Fuel consumption was measured during trials of four hours duration, each at a steady horsepower. After making adjustments for the maximum sea-going auxiliary load likely to be met on service, the fuel consumption is estimated to be about 47 tons/day at 2,800 shp and 117 tons/day at 12,000 shp.

In the load condition carrying 330 tons of oil fuel the endurance will be about 2,100 miles at 20 knots and 2,400 miles at the economical speed of 15 knots, with clean bottom.

Using extra fuel tank capacity available for long ocean passages and carrying 490 tons of oil fuel the endurance is increased to approximately 3,100 miles at 20 knots and 3,560 miles at 15 knots.

PLANS

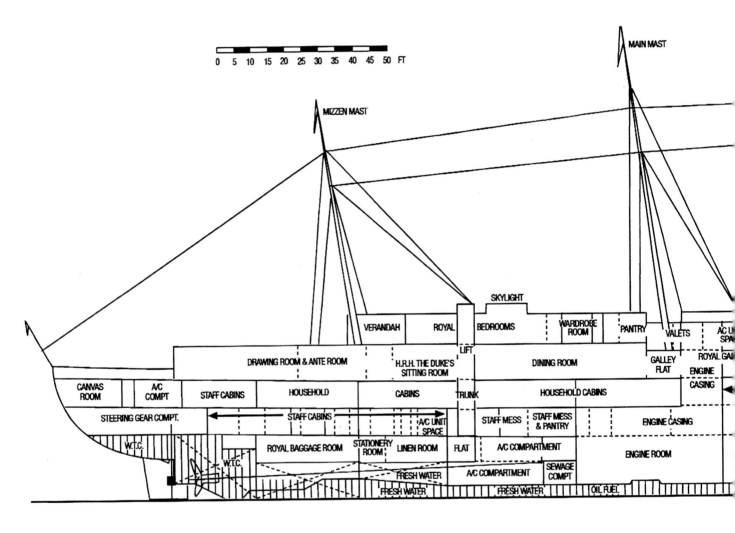

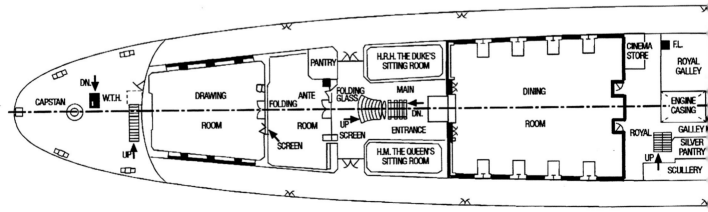

H.M. YACHT BRITANNIA. PROFILE

Plans drawn by Peter Gill & Associates

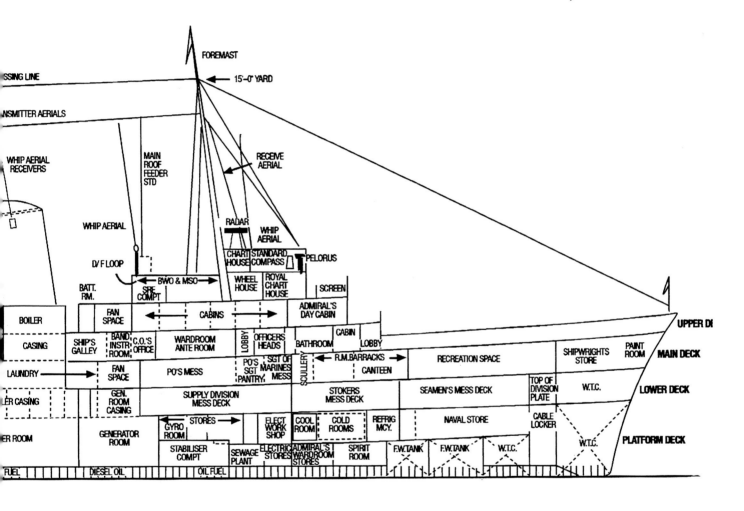

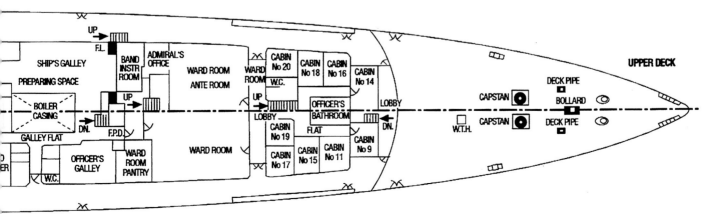

PRINCIPAL DIMENSIONS

Length overall	412-ft 3-in (125.65)
Length on waterline	380-ft 0-in
Length between perpendiculars	360-ft 0-in
Maximum breadth moulded	55-ft 0-in
Breadths at upper deck moulded	54-ft 6-in
Depth moulded to upper deck 45-ft abaft midships	32-ft 6-in
Depth moulded to upper deck at fore perpendicular	40-ft 4-in
Depth moulded to upper deck at after perpendicular	33-ft 10-in
Load displacement	4,715 tons
Mean draft at load displacement	15-ft 7$\frac{1}{2}$-in (5.2m)
Gross tonnage	5,862 tons
Shaft horsepower	12,000
Continuous sea-going speed	21 knots

MASTS	HEIGHT ABOVE U.S.K. TO TOP OF AERIALS	RAKE
Fore Mast	133-ft 0-in	1 per ft
Main Mast	139-ft 3-in	1 per ft
Mizzen Mast	118-ft 10-in	1 per ft

FUEL & WATER

330 tons of fuel oil providing a range of 2,000 miles at 20 knots.
120 tons of fresh water.
Additional tanks can increase fuel capacity to 490 tons and fresh water capacity to 195 tons.

PROPELLERS & RUDDER

Four-bladed propeller

Diameter	10-ft 3-ins
Pitch	9.0-ft
Developed blade area	55.7-sq ft
Tip clearance from hull	2-ft 9-in

Rudder

Maximum rudder torque 125 tons ft at 14 knots astern and 30$\frac{1}{2}$ deg angle.
Torque at 22 knots 69 tons ft at 35 deg angle.
Torque at 15 knots 33 tons ft at 35 deg angle.
Maximum normal rudder force 63.5 tons at 22 knots ahead, and 25.5 tons at 14 knots astern.

RUNNING AND MAINTENANCE COSTS

THE TOTAL COSTS of running *Britannia* during the past decade are as follows and include direct running, maintenance and pay:

	Millions
1984–85	£5.8
1985–86	£6.9
1986–87	£4.7
1987–88	* £22.4
1988–89	£9.5
1989–90	£7.0
1990–91	£9.3
1991–92	** £12.5
1992–93	£8.4
1993–94	£9.2
Total	£95.7

* The figure for 1987-88 includes £17 million for a major refit.

**The figure for 1991-92 includes £7.1 million for docking and repairs.

Routine maintenance and running costs up to the decommissioning year of 1997 were of the same order as those listed above.

Flag Officers Royal Yachts, 1954–1997

H.M.Y. BRITANNIA

Vice-Admiral Sir Connolly Abel-Smith, KCVO, CB	1954–58
Vice-Admiral Sir Peter Dawnay, KCVO, CB, DSC	1958–62
Rear-Admiral Sir Joseph Henley KCVO, CB	1962–65
Rear-Admiral Sir Patrick Morgan KCVO, CB, DSC	1965–70
Rear-Admiral Sir Richard Trowbridge KCVO	1970–75
Rear-Admiral Sir Hugh Janion KCVO	1975–81
Rear-Admiral Sir Paul Greening GCVO	1981–85
Rear-Admiral Sir John Garnier KCVO, CBE	1985–90
Rear-Admiral Sir Robert Woodard KCVO	1990–95

COMMODORE ROYAL YACHTS

Commodore Anthony Morrow CBE	1995–97

ROYAL RACING YACHTS

DURING THE THREE centuries since Royal Yachts were first introduced to Britain, there have been four periods when yachts were used not only as a means of transport but also for sport.

Yacht racing first became a Royal favourite during the reign of Charles II when, following the Restoration in 1660, he and his brother the Duke of York frequently raced their yachts for large wagers. Records show that this pastime lasted for about ten years.

The second period when yacht racing became popular among Royalty was in the 19th century, by which time Cowes, on the Isle of Wight, had become the mecca for international yachtsmen for one week in August. The Prince of Wales (later Edward VII) was the first member of the Royal Family to compete there. His first racing yacht, in 1866, was the *Dagmar*. During the next 20 years he owned and raced seven yachts. In 1869 he bought the *Princess,* and in 1871 the *Alexandra*, named after his wife. A year later *Zenobia* was purchased, followed by *Hildegarde* in 1876, *Formosa* in 1880, and *Aline* in 1882.

It was in 1892, when he became Commodore of the Royal Yacht Squadron, that the Prince of Wales commissioned G.L. Watson, one of the world's most eminent yacht designers, to build him a cutter, which became *Britannia*, the best-known racing yacht of her time. *Britannia* was the most successful of all the Prince's yachts, winning 157 races, before being sold in 1897. His Royal Highness – seeing her triumph in other hands – then bought her back two years later, sold her again in 1900, and finally, by now having acceded to the throne as King Edward VII, bought her for the third time in 1902. When King George V succeeded his father he also inherited an enthusiasm for the sport.

Britannia was brought out of retirement in 1919, after the First World War, and raced under the King's name until 1935. When he died the following year she was stripped of her equipment and sunk in the English Channel.

The fourth period blossomed under Prince Philip, who has never lost his enthusiasm for racing – or for Cowes Week. The yachts had become smaller and more economical, and Prince Philip showed his prowess with his Dragon class *Bluebottle*, and later with *Coweslip*, a Flying Fifteen. His Royal Highness encouraged his children to sail competitively, and the Princess Royal in particular has taken an active interest, being patron or member of a number of yacht squadrons.

THE PAYING-OFF CEREMONY, 11 DECEMBER 1997

BUCKINGHAM PALACE

Together with members of my family, Prince Philip and I join you today to pay tribute to BRITANNIA and give our thanks to all who have been part of her Company. Looking back over forty-four years we can all reflect with pride and gratitude upon this great ship which has served the country, the Royal Navy and my family with such distinction. BRITANNIA has provided magnificent support to us throughout this time, playing such an important role in the history of the second half of this century. Steaming over one million miles she has proudly carried out over seven hundred Royal visits at home and overseas as well as numerous highly successful commercial programmes. Her achievements are a great testament to those who designed and built her and to those craftsmen and artisans who have maintained her with such dedication over all these years.

In recognising BRITANNIA's marvellous service, we pay particular tribute to the Officers and Royal Yachtsmen who have served in her. My family and I extend our heartfelt thanks to all these men for their unfailing loyalty, dedication and commitment to the Royal Yacht Service. While many of the present Royal Yacht's Company will return to the Royal Navy to continue their naval service and others come to the end of their service, we wish you every success in your future endeavours. We would also wish to thank the wives and families who have quietly but strongly supported the Royal Yacht over the years and often during the periods of long absence.

It is with sadness that we must now say goodbye to BRITANNIA. It is appropriate that with this final event she bows out in the style which is so typical of the manner in which her business has always been conducted.

Elizabeth R *Philip*

11th December 1997.

THE PAYING-OFF FOR

HER MAJESTY'S YACHT BRITANNIA

on 11 December 1997 at 1500
in the presence of

Her Majesty The Queen and
His Royal Highness The Duke of
   Edinburgh and

H.R.H. The Prince of Wales
H.R.H. The Duke of York
H.R.H. The Prince Edward
H.R.H. The Princess Royal and
   Captain Timothy Laurence, Royal Navy
H.R.H. The Duke of Gloucester and
   H.R.H. The Duchess of Gloucester
H.R.H. The Duke of Kent
H.R.H. Prince Michael of Kent and
   H.R.H. Princess Michael of Kent
H.R.H. The Princess Alexandra, the Hon.
   Lady Ogilvy and
   The Rt. Hon. Sir Angus Ogilvy

BEAT RETREAT

Programme of Music

Per Mare Per Terram	Rose
Globe and Laurel	Dunn
Shrewsbury Fair	Neville

Ceremonial Drum Beatings by
   the Corps of Drums

Famous Songs of the British Isles	Dunn

Finale

Highland Cathedral	Korb
Sunset	Green
Rule Britannia	Arne
National Anthem	

March Past of the Royal Navy

Heart of Oak	Boyce

The Regimental March of
   HM Royal Marines

A Life On The Ocean Wave	Russell

LIST OF OFFICERS

Commodore	Anthony Morrow	Commodore Royal Yachts
Commander	Simon Martin	Executive Officer
Commander	Rupert Head	Commodore's Secretary and Supply Officer
Commander	Robin Parry	Engineer Officer
Surgeon Commander	Alistair Neal	Principal Medical Officer
Commander	Jeremy Blunden	Navigating Officer
Captain, Royal Marines	David Cole	Director of Music
Lieutenant Commander	Tim Stockings	First Lieutenant
Lieutenant Commander	Michael O'Riordan	Second Lieutenant
Lieutenant Commander	Paul Gorsuch	Deputy Supply Officer
Lieutenant Commander	Richard Randall	Senior Engineer
Lieutenant Commander	Barry Llewelyn	Keeper and Steward of the Royal Apartments
Lieutenant Commander	Nigel Chandler	Communications Officer and Flag Lieutenant
Lieutenant	Julian Philo	Electrical Officer
Lieutenant	Mark Pomeroy	Main Machinery Officer
Lieutenant	Louis Jordan	Hull Services Officer
Lieutenant	Jack Kerr	Boatswain
Lieutenant	Christopher Hocking	Household Liaison Officer
Lieutenant	Howard Bailey	Assistant Navigating Officer

YACHT'S COMPANY

WOMEA (P)	D M Smith
WOWTR	R E White
CCMEA (L)	P G H Adams
BANDMASTER	D J Bromley
MR (NAAFI MANAGER)	S R Cooper
CCMEA	J G Mace
CCMEA (H)	G J Smissen
CCMT	A M Travis
CPOCA	N P Allan
CPOMEA (ML)	S N Barlow
CPOMEA (EL)	A C Baxter
CPOMEA (M)	V J Blake
CPOSTD	D J Bond
CPOMEM (M)	D H Bosomworth
CPOCA	A K Dick
CPOWEM (R)	M A Downer
CPOSTD	G K Easter
CPO (SEA)	A R Francis
CPOCA	D J French
CPOMEA (ML)	D W Henery
CPOSTD	S J Hope
CPOMEA (H)	A G Jefferies
CPOMEA (ML)	R P Kernaghan
CPOWEA	R Lapworth
D/MAJ	G I Naylor
CPOMEM (M)	M Peet
CCY	C I Plows
CPOMEA (ML)	N A Royle
CPOMA	A M Shenton
CRS	N R Sullivan
BDCSGT	W G Tate
CPOMEM (L)	J K Turner
CPOMEA (P)	J D B Utterson
CPO (S)	P D R Young
PO (SEA)	J C Allen
BSGT	P Beal
PO (SEA)	M J Bennett
POCA	M S D Boswell
POCA	D G Byles
POMEM (M)	G E Charman
POMEM (M)	M L Currell
POCY	M D Gentry
POMEM (M)	D W Gibbs
POMEM (M)	A J Graham
POSTD	S F Green
POMEM (M)	L P Greening
LCSGT	D Griffiths
POMEM (L)	W F Harding
RS	P Hook
POSA	H W Horne
PO (M)	A Ingram
BDSGT	P Johnson

Rank	Name	Rank	Name	Rank	Name
PO (R)	G F Kettle	LMEM (L)	A B Miskin	MEM (M) 1	S P Hamid
POMEM (M)	A K King	LRO (G)	D D Moss	MEM (M) 1	G M Harrop
LBDSGT	D T Matthews	LCH	B P Mutimer	AB (R)	N Hembury
POMEM (M)	J Patterson	LMEM (M)	A D Nicol	MUSN	C W Henderson
RS	P M Powell	LMEM (M)	K P Norman	MNE 1	M Herron
POMEM (M)	D T Rayner	LMEM (M)	D W O'Brien	MEM (M) 1	R A Hunt
POSTD	D C Rowe	LSTD	G Oram	AB (R)	P R Inglesby
L/SGTBUG	A P Travis	LSTD	A P Pasker	MUSN	N C Jackson
POPT	A Tutchings	LSTD	R Pitt	AB (R)	M D S James
POSA	A B P Wheeler	LCH	J L Postello	BUG	D R James
POWEA	D I Wilson	LMEM (L)	A J Pugsley	MEM (M) 1	M C Jays
POMEM (L)	B J Winstone	LRO (T)	M J Rider	STD	A J Jones
PO (MW) (O)	P E Yates	LSTD	P Roddis	AB (MW)	R J Kennedy
LSEA (R)	R I Abbott	LRO (G)	T P Walsh	AB (R)	S J Kiernan
LCH	C J Anderson	LS (M)	D J Wharram	MNE 1	J A Kilday
BDCPL	M S Andrew	LWTR	P C Whittaker	AB (R)	N King
LCH	C L Angove	LMEM (L)	D Williams	MEM (M) 1	G R S Kitchenham
LSTD	N A Ashton	LS (R)	N Wolstenholme	STD	I T Lewis
BDCPL	E C Bean	LMEM (M)	R K Wood	MEM (M) 1	W H Mainland
LSTD	D T Bell	LRO (T)	S P Wright	RO (G) 1	P L McCraw
CPL/BUG	C J Boulton	CPL	T M Wright	AB (S)	M F McGinty
LMEM (M)	G J Boyd	AB (S)	D J Avis	MEM (M) 1	C McLocklan
LMEM (L)	R J Brooman	WTR	J S Barlow	AB (M)	S J Miller
BDCPL	M R Buxton	STD	A W Barnes	STD	N W Miller
LMEM (L)	A S Callaghan	MEM (M) 1	D C Beever	AB (R)	D S Moore
LRO	A D Carter	AB (MW)	R I Bell	RO 1	A J Moreton
LS (M)	P B Caws	MEM (M) 1	M P Birchall	RO (T)	G S Morley
LRO (T)	A P Cobb	RO (G)	G Bisset	MUSN	W H Morris
LCH	J P Connor	AB (S)	G W Blake	MUSN	J D Moss
LS (SEA)	K N Cottingham	MEM (M) 1	R D C Bugg	AB (S)	M A A O'Brien
BDCPL	S P Cracknell	AB (M)	M P Calverley	AB (R)	S M Palmer
LCH	M J Crankshaw	AB (M)	N J Campion	MEM (M) 1	N E Plumbley
LSTD	M Crawford	CH	S Campion	AB (M)	J G Roberts
LCH	S C Dixey	STD	P Carmichael	MEM (M) 1	C J Rolfe
LS (R)	S J Edwards	AB (R)	M Carpenter	AB (S)	D P Roper
LSTD	M Elliott	MNE	M A Carron	RO (T)	M S Rushton
LMEM (M) 1	D G Fountain	AB (MW)	G K Cawthorne	MUSN	D J Scott
LRO (T)	P Frisby	BUG	A J Child	STD	D M Simpson
LSTD	M B Gander	MEM (M) 1	J R Christopher	AB (MW)	M R Smith
LMEM (M)	J A Gould	MNE	P E Cole	MEM (M) 1	E S Smyth
MR (NAAFI)	D Graham	MEM (M) 1	A M W Corbett	MEM (M) 1	B Spencer
LWTR	M T Grant	MUSN	N W Crompton	AB (R)	A P Stephenson
LS (M)	P A Hale	MEM (M) 1	N A Dednum	STD	W Strickland
LS (M)	L W Hammett	AB (S)	J R Dennis	AB (M)	W Sutherland
LMEM (M)	A S Harrison	AB (R)	S B Doughty	MUSN	P G Sykes
LS (M)	S E Hislop	CH	K A J Douglas	LRO (C)	M Thomson
LSTD	C P Hobbs	AB (M)	M S Duchesne	MNE	D J Tucker
LA (PHOT)	D Hunt	MEM (M) 1	S P Elks	MEM (M) 1	D Wagstaff
LCH	S F Leigh	MEM (M) 1	R D Ellis	AB (R)	T N Webster
LMEM (M)	A J Longhorn	MEM (M) 1	S D Field	MUSN	A J Williams
LSA	J Lovett	MEM (M) 1	C J Forbes	STD	M S Wood
LSTD	A T Marsh	MEM (L) 1	P A Found	MUSN	G A Wright
LMEM (M)	A Maytum	AB (R)	S V Fox	MUSN	J Z L Wright
BDCPL	P B Meacham	WEM (R)	D I Gallagher	MNE	M A Youngson
LMEM (M)	S Mearns	MEM (M) 1	S L Gane		
LMEM (M)	S Merrick		S M Grundy		

INDEX

H.M.Y. BRITANNIA